make it
happen

Jenna Herbut

make it happen

THE CREATIVE ENTREPRENEUR'S GUIDE TO **TRANSFORMING** YOUR **DREAMS** INTO **REALITY**

PAGE TWO
BOOKS

ISBN 978-0-9952665-3-7 (paperback)
ISBN 978-1-989025-23-9 (ebook)

Page Two Books
www.pagetwobooks.com
Cover design by Naomi MacDougall and Diana Luong
Interior design by Naomi MacDougall
Editing by Kendra Ward
Proofreading by Susan Traxel and Alison Strobel

Printed and bound in Canada by Friesens

18 19 20 21 22   5 4 3 2 1

Distributed in Canada by Raincoast Books
Distributed in the US and internationally by Publishers Group West, a division of Ingram

www.jennaherbut.com
www.makeitshow.ca

Contents

· · · · · · · · · · ·

This book is dedicated to past, present, and future Makies. It's an absolute privilege to be making it happen with you!

Trenna,

I've always loved our chats and I'm so grateful you're part of this community. Can't wait to see what you make happen next! Sparkly ♡
Love Jenn

A Note from the Author

. . . .

$\int$ wrote *Make It Happen* because I want to make it easier for people to design and create their own reality. To help take big, audacious ideas and make them real so that others can enjoy and benefit in their actualization. There's a lot of talk about making your dreams come true, but as glorious as this idea is, I personally didn't feel there were enough examples of women who've done it.

After many battles with my inner critic, I decided it was time for me to take a stand. It feels like the next step in my entrepreneurial journey; and although being seen as a "role model" scares the crap out of me, I knew it was time for me to share my entrepreneurial experience with the world. I also realized I am where I am today because of women like Oprah, Marie Forleo, and Sara Blakely. These are a few of my role models who've been extraordinary examples of how life can change form when you start to follow your inner guidance and think differently. It's because of these women standing proudly and owning their greatness that I feel I can do the same. If I can help you realize your dreams through sharing my own journey, it would be sad to think that fear and uncertainty might have held me back.

I am a product of my thoughts, beliefs, and habits (just like everyone else) so I wanted to write a book that shared these with other creative entrepreneurs. To write this book, I channelled "Little Jenna," who I was when I first had the impulse to make it happen. Maybe you see the world in a similar way, or maybe you see it through a different lens. Regardless, my hope is this book will be a positive influence on your path to fulfilling your desires.

To get a better understanding of the topic, I did countless hours of research on the subject of goal actualization, manifestation, and mindset. I'm not a psychologist, nor do I have any formal training in psychology. What I am is a creative entrepreneur who has worked with thousands of other creative entrepreneurs through the Make It craft fairs. My expertise in writing this book comes from observing behavioural patterns and having countless conversations with business owners from various backgrounds. From brave newbies in the early start-up stages, to a friend who sold his online dating business for over half a billion dollars, I've had the great privilege of profound conversations with folks at all stages of their business journeys.

To get to the level of success I'm currently experiencing, I've struggled, wobbled, and made a ton of mistakes! But as many wrong turns as I made (and continue to make today), I began to live by a mantra which is to "trust and surrender." By leaning in to the process and trusting that even the darkest days would eventually turn bright, I've learned to let go of things like outcomes and hard-set plans. I learned to embrace levity, fun, and joy as key aspects of business. At first it felt counterproductive because I had SO MUCH TO DO, but then I started to get a clear picture that there was something greater at work that had nothing to do with how many hours I put in.

I've often been asked the question: *What would you tell your former self that you know now?* There are many things that I sometimes wish I could whisper into Little Jenna's ear so the struggle wouldn't have been so painful. But the reality is the story you're about to read wouldn't be nearly as juicy if I didn't bang headfirst into as many walls as I did. I'm a product of my wins, as well as my losses. If I knew anything then that I know now, my life would be completely different and I might not have felt inspired to write this book.

Before you dive in, my suggestion is to open your heart and mind to your own potential. My belief, which has been substantiated many times throughout my research, is that we're all born with gifts which are endless seeds of possibility. I'm not sure if anyone has fully actualized them all (I certainly haven't), but I believe it's a noble act of bravery to at least try. It would be ignorant to think that we all come from the same background or upbringing, but as David Bowie reminded us, we're *all* made of stardust. My dream is for you to enjoy the absolute incredible thrill of making it happen. Trust me, the juice is worth the squeeze!

Yes, You Can!

. . . .

J'M SO HONOURED and thrilled that you were inspired to
pick up this book! It probably means that you have *big*,
exciting, glorious ideas that you want to turn into reality. Maybe you've had this longing for a while and it's finally
time to take action, or maybe your plan is something fresh
and new that recently popped into your head. Regardless,
making it happen has profound positive benefits, not only
for you but for everyone on the planet. The more you can
make your creative ideas a reality, the more exhilarating and
enjoyable your life will become. The key is to do the things
that light you up and to avoid doing things because of obligation or outside pressure. "Should" and "could" are never
compelling reasons to do anything great.

This book is for people who have dreams of making their
creative ideas a reality. Your ideas are seeds that you're ready
to plant and nurture as they grow—an amazing product or
a service that you want to offer the world. You may already
have had some success pursuing your idea. Maybe you've
started your business and things have been going pretty well

so far. From the outside, others might see you as a success—because you are one. If you're already on this journey, that's an amazing accomplishment and I'm so proud of you. Not many people have the guts to start, and getting over that initial hump is an achievement in itself. My hope is that you're also very proud of yourself.

Make It Happen is for the rare breed that wants to take life to the next level, making it even bigger and more extraordinary. Things may be going well already, but you know they could be *outstanding*. You know you're awesome and have an abundance of skills and abilities, but something seems to stop you from doing the thing that, deep down, you really want to do. This is something I know all too much about.

There have been many times when I've had a great idea, felt super-excited about it, told my closest friends and family, started, and shortly thereafter got stuck in quicksand. A few times, I spent a lot of money on new equipment and courses to keep myself accountable and committed. Even though I wanted to realize my goal, it was as though an invisible force was preventing me from rising up to the next level. I imagine you have a similar pattern and are as frustrated with it as I've felt with my own. It's a very common human experience. But I'm here to tell you that it doesn't have to be this way. Overcoming the biggest obstacles to our self-defined success—making it happen—is entirely possible. It doesn't mean resistance won't be there, because it will. But you'll have the tools to plough through it.

I wrote this book because I wanted to figure out what holds people back from making it happen and to offer a guide that could help others turn their brilliant ideas and dreams into reality. In the chapters ahead, you'll read stories about my own entrepreneurial journey—which has been wild and crazy at times—beginning with my earliest business endeavours as a child; to my first "real" business (an accessory line called Booty Beltz); to my founding of Make It, one of Canada's largest craft fairs. You'll also read stories about people I've come to know through the Make It community. These courageous badasses offer shining examples of how to do the thing you've always wanted to do. Though they come from different backgrounds and industries, they're linked because they've realized their dreams—despite fear, resistance, negativity from family and friends, and all the nasty stuff that can trip us up and cause us to quit before we make it happen. I share all this with you because I want you to know that if others can make it happen, so can you!

In each chapter, you'll discover a different aspect of making it happen and exercises to assist you in applying the principles of this book. Please also visit jennaherbut.com, for interviews, resources, and online courses designed to support you as you move further along this path.

Anything is possible if you go about it with the right mindset. People give up on their big dreams because they bump up against something sticky and uncomfortable within themselves, and instead of busting through, they succumb to the resistance. It hurts my heart to think of all the amazing ideas that never come to fruition because of this sad fact. Who knows, maybe there would be flying cars, everlasting gobstoppers, and world peace if, rather than letting go of their brilliant ideas, people found the inner resources to make it happen!

You've picked up this book because you recognize your own potential and splendour. If you were an unmotivated slacker, you would have been turned off already and be on the couch, binge-watching Netflix. I can help you make it happen only if you already have a burning desire. *Make It Happen* is for the dreamers, the visionaries, and the believers. You have all the magical stuff inside you, but through these pages we may tweak your vision so that you see more clearly how amazing you really are. When you can see your own magnificence, you become a force of nature and those sneaky thoughts and beliefs that used to get in your way don't stand a chance.

Use this book as your partner in crime as you become the masterful creative genius you truly are. Allow it to help remove the resistance that keeps you from doing what you were put on Earth to do. The more you shine, the greater the light in the world and a better place it will be for us all.

I suggest that you begin by signing the pledge, committing yourself to this process no matter how uncomfortable it might sometimes feel. This signed pledge will function like a permission slip for moving forward, and I guarantee that you won't be the same afterward. Renowned life coach and entrepreneur Tony Robbins says that if you want to take the island, you have to burn the boats. To do great things in the world, you must draw a line in the sand and make a commitment. If you're ready to truly step up to the next level of life, sign your name as a declaration to live your best life.

By signing and dating the pledge, you are committing to yourself that you will make it happen, despite how strong the resistance might be along your journey. For bonus points, call or text your best friends and tell them about your commitment. If you're really brave, post on social media about your commitment to finally realize your next big dream.

Make sure you tag @jennaherbut on Instagram so I can follow along with your exciting progress.

After you sign, take a deep breath, be fully present in the moment, and don't look back. I'll see you on the other side.

Sparkly love,
Jenna

BY SIGNING BELOW,
I'M COMMITTING MYSELF TO
MAKE IT HAPPEN.

_____

NAME

_____

TODAY'S DATE

Part One

. . . .

WHAT WILL YOU MAKE HAPPEN?

one

Committing to Yourself

· ·

"There are three kinds of people in this world: people who make it happen, people who watch what happens, and people who wonder what happened."

TOMMY LASORDA

YOU'VE MADE A commitment to yourself to begin this journey! I am so proud of you. Within you, right now, is everything you need to achieve anything you want, and I'm here to convince you of that, so you can see it manifest in your life. Through research and by looking at my own life, I've been able to change how my brain works. Things that used to scare me and trip me up no longer get in my way like they did before. I still deal with resistance and challenges, but I have the awareness to move through them more efficiently than I used to. My intention is for you to be able to see my experience, and that of the people interviewed for this book, as proof and confirmation that you can make it happen too. The desire to manifest your dreams will never stop, and learning how to create them effectively will give you a taste of what's possible: *anything!*

In addition to signing the pledge to yourself, you must make a few other commitments so that what you learn in this book will have the biggest possible impact.

If you're a somewhat rebellious entrepreneur who lives by your own rules, you might be like me. I hate being told what to do and generally resist authority, so I have to check in with myself regularly to understand what causes me to react that way. Usually, when I'm reluctant to do something, it's because my ego is making a fuss, because it fears the unknown. I guarantee that your ego will speak up—and may even get belligerent—while you're reading this book.

One of the most important perspectives you can have is that of a witness. I have trained myself to practise taking a step back and observing what triggers me whenever I strongly feel something. Usually it's my ego trying desperately to keep me small so that I feel safe. The ego is designed to keep us secure, so it often acts up when something unfamiliar is present. Keeping us out of harm's way can be incredibly helpful in the right context.

But this is *not* that time. When you're making it happen you bust through limiting beliefs and change your brain chemistry as a result. The ego will go crazy, and your job is to acknowledge it but not let it steer the ship. You must be the one in charge of your ego, teaching it to bow down to your authentic greatness. This might seem esoteric, but trust me, you'll understand what I'm talking about as we move forward with the make it happen process.

Here are some thoughts, feelings, and sensations you might encounter as you read this book:

1. *Thinking that you know this stuff already.* I've had this reaction many times while reading books and sitting in workshops. When I was in school, this attitude would get me in trouble! But when I think that I already know something, it's usually my ego holding me back by blocking out experiences that could be useful. Zen Buddhism uses the term *shoshin*, which means "beginner's mind." It refers to an attitude of keen openness and a lack of preconceptions when studying a subject. Taking on this useful perspective allows you to absorb new information without judgement. You never know what's coming. When you judge, you block something that could be very important from entering your life and allowing you to have a miraculous shift. The beginner's mind is receptive and expansive and exactly the muscle that needs to be developed to make it happen.

2. *Thinking that none of this applies to you.* This sounds a lot like point one, but it's slightly different. When you're dealing with ego resistance, you'll likely discount ideas and information so that you can feel safe in life as it is. Closing ourselves off feels less risky than letting the new in. It's easier to just discount something than it is to try it on and experience it. Here's an example: as a kid, I hated mushrooms. My mom used to tell me my palate wasn't sophisticated enough to handle their flavour and appreciate their consistency. I refused to eat them for many years and would complain about having to pick them out of my food. Then, one day, I decided to try them again. To my surprise, I enjoyed eating them, and now I eat mushrooms often. It's as if my taste buds suddenly

understood how to process the complexity of the flavours on my palate. If I continued to have the belief that I didn't want anything to do with mushrooms, I'd be missing out on many yummy experiences.

3. *Feeling like trying it on takes too much time.* I love to read and always have a book next to my bed. It's probably not shocking to hear that I gravitate toward reading self-help books. For a long time, I would read these books but not do any of the exercises. I would mentally rehearse them, but I wouldn't pull out my journal and do the work. When I decided that I was ready to shift that limiting behaviour, everything I read became much more beneficial. As you're reading this book, there will be times when I ask you to do something that you won't want to do. It's okay to slack and cut yourself a break some of the time, but just realize that this is likely the very thing that's holding you back from making it happen. The ego loves to convince you to not do exactly what will make the biggest difference.

4. *Feeling like it's all too much and you can't do it.* You're absolutely going to feel this way as you read this book. If you don't, you likely aren't reaching high enough. I have wanted to stop pretty much everything I've started, no matter how badly I wanted to make it happen at first. Don't fret if this comes up for you, because it will. You might feel the resistance in your mind and also in your body. For me, "too much" is a heavy, nagging, uncomfortable sensation in my chest and solar plexus. In the past, I've pushed this feeling away to make it stop. Because I'm operating with more awareness now, I

embrace it, breathe into it, and lovingly release it. It's not always easy, and sometimes I can't fully let it go, but continual practice has made me *way* better at it. Once you bust through your own overwhelm, you'll find so much waiting for you on the other side of it.

Other thoughts, feelings, and sensations will be present when you read this book, but for now I want you to start identifying those four, which I believe hold the tightest grip. This book is intended to inspire you into action and it will work for you if you work with it. Think of it as a beautiful partnership rather than another thing you have to do. Commit to doing the exercises to make it happen and things will start to shift and open for you. The legendary Wayne Dyer once said that "when you believe it, you'll see it." Most people think the opposite, so they're always waiting for amazing things to show up in their lives to prove what's possible. If you can shift your thinking, a whole new magical world will open up to you.

Committing to something fully is exciting and terrifying—or, as I like to call it, *excitifying*! When you decide to make change in your life, there's no going back, and you start to think and feel differently as a result. People take notice, and not everyone is going to like it. Some, perhaps those closest to you, will miss the old you. This can feel very strange and uncomfortable, but keep reminding yourself that this is *your* life and people who try to stop you from making progress could be threatened because they feel it's not possible for themselves. When you make your dreams the priority, things start to happen effortlessly. We'll be exploring this idea in much more detail later in the book, but for now know that ease comes when you make a commitment to yourself. This is not an easy thing to do, which is why not a lot of people truly embrace commitment.

The Make It Real exercises that conclude each chapter are an opportunity to put ideas into action. Without proactive steps forward, you'll never get your desired results, no matter how much you meditate on or visualize the outcome.

Let's take some action right now. Below is the first set of exercises to get this party started! Please use a journal—so that you can look back at your progress and realize how far you've come. Your journal will be part of your bigger picture and help you in ways you can't even know yet—that's how powerful journaling is. As with anything, do your best and don't worry about being perfect or doing it the "right" way. This journey is all about you. No one else is going to read your journal unless you share it.

Make It Real
. . . .

In your journal, put your pen to paper and allow a stream of consciousness to flow as you fully respond to each of the following questions.

1. What thoughts of resistance have already come up for you? For example, do you think this book will be a waste of time or that you already know how to do this on your own? Whatever nasty little negative thoughts come up, write them down immediately, without judgement.

2. What have you resisted, or even hated, in the past that you enjoy now? Write a list of things for which your tastes have changed and recall what caused the shift from dislike to like, or even love.

3. In the past five years, what habits that you committed to cultivating have stuck? Did you start a new exercise routine or a new diet that feels effortless now? What did you do to make these new behaviours part of your life? Note the methods that worked best for you so that you can apply them to making it happen.

4. Do you have any deeply rooted, repetitive thoughts about why in the past you haven't been able to make it happen? Sometimes it's painful to admit to ourselves the true reason our lives aren't the way we'd like them to be. But there's a lot of power in truth, so the clearer you are about what stops you, the easier it will be to bust through those limitations. If this starts to feel heavy, take a deep breath and remember that you're not your past and it's possible to change any behaviour pattern when you have self-awareness and the right tools.

two

My Story of Making It Happen

. . . .

"Private dreams are the most powerful. You have to
dream of success to make it happen, and if you don't
believe in yourself, nobody else will. But that doesn't mean
you have to go around telling everyone about it."

TONY MCCOY

EVERY SUCCESSFUL CREATIVE person I've spoken with
has shared a similar experience: being a pioneer can
feel very lonely because not a lot of people know what
you're going through. I've felt pain and discomfort while I've
been making it happen at times when I didn't have a strong
support system. It took me years to cultivate that, and sometimes I still struggle with feeling isolated. This is why I'm
sharing my story with you: because I know you'll see yourself in it. I want to reassure you that you are not alone on
this journey—even though at points it might feel as though
you are.

Steve Jobs said, "You can't connect the dots looking forward; you can only connect them looking backwards. So you

have to trust that the dots will somehow connect in your future." I've had some pretty crazy (and amusing) experiences that have allowed me to get to a point where I can see how my life has unfolded, and continues to, all in my favour. It doesn't always feel this way in the moment, but I try my best to see the lessons.

I'm sharing my story with you in the hope that as you read it, you'll trace your own beginnings as a creative entrepreneur, viewing your journey through a lens of compassion and appreciation for all that you've experienced to get to this precise moment. Maybe you also have some hilarious stories from childhood of starting your own little business to warmly reflect on!

Now, please join me as I take you back to where my make it happen journey all began.

The Bookmark Biz

I started my entrepreneurial journey, accidentally, at a very young age. Growing up, I always loved crafting, and art was my favourite subject in school. I enjoyed moulding pipe cleaners, glue, sparkles—and anything else—into something that had never been seen or done before. Using my imagination, I could make anything I wanted. This was an incredible feeling of freedom.

It didn't take long for me to realize that I also had a strong entrepreneurial spirit. The idea of selling something I had made mesmerized me. More than anything, I loved to make money. I was never hard done by as a kid, but I *was* obsessed with selling my crafts for cash!

The first "real" business I created was in the early '90s. I was 11 years old and my brother, Chandler, was almost 9.

My school supplies were the wackiest, brightest, and funkiest I could possibly find. One day, I decided to make bookmarks out of some jazzy-looking dividers, so with my scissors, my hole puncher, and some yarn to make a pompom—because these were going to be legit bookmarks, after all—I made prototypes for my mom, dad, little brother, and me. Then I thought, *Why not take these bookmarks to the masses?* Soon enough, Chandler and I were producing them factory style.

After churning out a ton of bookmarks, it was time to take action and start selling. As kids, we didn't have a lot of options for sales channels. We couldn't drive anywhere by ourselves, and I thought my mom would be skeptical of the idea, so I didn't want to enlist her help until we had proven we could do it.

But *how* would we do it? I asked myself: *What is the best way to get these babies into the books of readers everywhere?* The Girl Guides flashed through my mind. My parents often bought their cookies when they came door to door. I decided that our best course of action was to take to the streets of Edmonton, Alberta, and bring the bookmarks to the people. I found a shoebox and stuffed the bookmarks inside, made a sign, grabbed young Chandler, and off we went.

I had no structured plan for carrying out this operation, and there were butterflies in my stomach as we approached the first house in our neighbourhood. After giving Chandler a quick pep talk and taking a few deep breaths, I pressed the doorbell. A few moments later, Mrs. Stanley answered the door. My brother and her son were friends, and she greeted us with a smile. After saying hello, I opened my box of bookmarks and asked if she would like to buy a few.

When she asked how much they cost, I panicked. A price! I had never considered that. I just loved making bookmarks and wanted people to give me money for them. I blurted out the first thing that came into my head: 75 cents or a $1? Thoughtfully, Mrs. Stanley asked why there were two different prices. Hmmm, I had no idea. She then asked if I would like some advice. I nodded enthusiastically. Customers always want to pay the lowest amount, she told me, so I should figure out a price that covered my costs but still allowed me to make money. Wow. She had my attention now. In the end, she bought two—probably because she felt obliged, and also, hopefully, because she wanted an exceptionally funky bookmark.

LESSONS LEARNED

- Always figure out your price ahead of time. Also, if someone doesn't like your product, just go to the next door—because there's a good chance someone else will.

Glow-in-the-Dark Shows

I produced my first event when I was 12 years old. I was into dance and theatre, and I loved the performing arts. Seeing *The Phantom of the Opera* with my mom, for example, was a transformational experience. That professional Broadway show rocked my soul, and I listened to *The Phantom of the Opera* CD over and over again. I would relive the amazing performances and dream about being on a big stage someday.

It was still the early '90s, and glow-in-the-dark items were all the rage. I stuck little plastic stars all over my ceiling, wore my groovy glow-in-the-dark Keds, and even had a few pieces of clothing that lit up under the cloak of darkness. Chandler had Construx and other toys that glowed when the lights went out.

Chandler and I were good friends with the kids who lived across the street, a family of three boys close to our age. We played with them a lot, although being the only girl, I often felt outnumbered. But I was also the oldest and most bossy, so I usually got my way.

One day, while thinking of my beloved *Phantom*, I decided to make my own play. I pitched my idea to the boys. They were totally confused and probably thought I was crazy, *at first*. But I was pretty persuasive, even back then. I realized I would have to perform the role of any good director and boss them around until I got what I wanted. Or at least that's what my instincts told me. We would use our friends' basement as a stage, and I would choreograph. After all, I took dance classes, so I knew all about it. But the pièce de résistance would be that we'd do it all glow-in-the-dark. The boys went along with it, probably because I told them that they'd make some money, and once the show was solid enough to share with the public (in other words, our parents) we would sell tickets for it. Naturally, we'd also provide snacks— shopped from our parents' pantries—available for purchase. I know, I know. That's pretty shady. But please know, I was a straight-A student with mostly good morals and values. I was just romanced by the idea of making money.

After selling tickets to our parents and neighbours (including Mrs. Stanley, who bought our bookmarks), we were ready to show off all our hard work. I really wish someone had recorded our performance. Imagine four boys under the age of 12 dancing around in glow-in-the-dark clothing while using Construx and other toys as props. It was a spectacular, eclectic combination of dance, acrobatics, and making shit up on the spot.

The boys came through for me, and we divided the profits equally. Despite being a bit shady, I believed in equal pay. As for the stolen snacks, my parents were not overly thrilled, but I'm pretty sure they were a little impressed by my ingenuity.

LESSON LEARNED

- You have to help others see your vision so that they'll help you execute it.

Refreshments at the 14th Hole

My family lived on the 14th hole of a golf course in Edmonton. My parents and brother were big golfers, and I also played, mostly because I didn't have a choice. But living on a golf course provided my brother and me with some exciting entrepreneurial opportunities. A couple of times each summer, we would trek down deep into the ravines and collect dozens of golf balls that had been mis-hit off the tee box. We'd load our backpacks with these treasures and take them home to clean them with soapy water. My parents were big supporters of this routine because they never had to buy golf balls.

One summer day, inspiration hit. We had more balls than my family could ever hope to use, so wouldn't it make sense to sell them back to the golfers? Plus, since we lived on one of the holes, we could just set up a little stand right along the fence. I convinced Chandler of my brilliant concept, found an old table in our garage, and with my neatest penmanship created a sign that read "$1/ball." The next morning, we set up shop.

Our first day was slow. Many of the golfers told us they already had enough balls in their bags and didn't need any more. Hmmm, I thought. If they didn't need more balls, maybe they needed something else. Knowing that after the first nine holes my dad would invariably stop by the snack shack for refreshments, I thought, *That's it!* We would sell cold drinks. At the 14th hole, the golfers would be finished the drinks they bought at the ninth and would be happy to buy more. So the next day, I hauled out a cooler, filled it with ice cubes, and then searched my family's pantry. There were bottles of water, cans of Coke, and beer. Perfect. All the basics covered. Since golf balls were going for $1, it made sense to ask the same price for the drinks.

It didn't take us long to rack up the sales. We were feeling pretty good about ourselves—until our parents caught on to our scheme. When my dad came home from work and took off his suit, he asked my mom where all the beer had gone. She had no idea. I knew in the long run I would only be in more trouble if I didn't come clean, so I told them what Chandler and I had been up to earlier in the day. My dad was simultaneously mad and impressed. He's an entrepreneur himself, so I'm sure he appreciated the hustle. But when he asked me how much we charged for the drinks, I got another lesson about profit margins.

LESSONS LEARNED

• No money can be made if you sell something for less than it's worth. And, if you have an entrepreneurial spirit, it just needs to be expressed.

Jenna's Jewellery Co.

Jewellery is something I've always been crazy for, so it was only natural that eventually I would be inspired to make my own. As a kid, I loved going to bead stores. I would pester my mom to take me to them so that I could stock up on colourful seed beads and fishing line. At one point, I had so many little plastic containers that I could have made necklaces for my entire school! I spent every last dime of my allowance money on my bead obsession, but I was truly happy.

After making a bazillion necklaces, bracelets, and anklets, I needed to start moving them onto the necks, wrists, and ankles of others. One brave day, I packed my bag with a few of my best pieces and visited a cute consignment store in downtown Edmonton. The owner seemed sweet, so I asked her if she would be interested in buying some of my jewellery. I was in high school by then and my sales skills were slightly more sophisticated than in my bookmark days. She thought my sample items were cute and she was interested in selling them on consignment. My heart leaped in my chest! A store was going to sell my jewellery! I felt like my dreams had come true. She suggested I come back with anything I wanted to sell, along with an order form to track everything.

Order form. That was a foreign term in my 16-year-old vocabulary. Luckily, my business-guy dad gave me insight into how to create such a thing. But first, he told me, I needed to think of a name for my business. Shit was getting real.

I decided on Jenna's Jewellery Co. Not the most original thing I've ever come up with, but I didn't know much about marketing and branding in those days. My dad then told me I needed to create a logo. Keep in mind it was the late '90s and today's sophisticated logo-making software wasn't readily available. So I clicked around in Microsoft Word until I found a font I liked and surfed the web until I located an order form template. Then, with the help of scissors and glue, I merged the two the old-fashioned way. My dad took the crafty order form to work and made copies of it. They looked almost legit.

Holding in my hands these makeshift order forms thrilled me to bits. Something about seeing my business name in type was overwhelmingly exciting. It felt real. When I dropped off my first order of Jenna's Jewellery, my heart swelled with pride. In that moment, I knew this was what I was meant to be doing. It just felt so right.

The sales of Jenna's Jewellery were not as gangbusters as I had hoped they would be, but the experience taught me so much. I got to know the woman who owned the store and she gave me a lot of useful advice about being a manufac-turer. She offered me tips on packaging, pricing, and how to follow trends. Looking back, I have a lot of gratitude for her taking a chance on me. My jewellery wasn't overly amazing, but I realize now she probably saw something in me. Whatever it was, it gave me a real taste of what was to come.

A FEW MONTHS later, I was with my best friend at HUB, the University of Alberta mall. Her father owned a drugstore there and, still in high school, we felt very cool to be hanging out around university kids after school. One of the stores sold hemp jewellery. It was all the rage back then and I wore many woven bracelets adorned with FIMO beads (remember those?!) and my mom had taught me how to work the beads into macramé. I admired the store and shopped there every time I was at HUB.

One day, I decided to be bold and talk to the store owner about my new business. To my surprise, he was very interested and presented me with a unique offer. He would give me a bunch of FIMO beads if I would create necklaces and bracelets with them. He would then buy the jewellery back from me for $3 apiece. My eyes must have bugged out of my head at this amazing opportunity.

After stocking up on loads of hemp, I began to macramé up a storm. I had nimble fingers and a strong desire to make cash, so it didn't take me long to produce a nice supply to bring back to the store. The owner seemed impressed with my skills and gave me more beads.

Because I was so motivated to make money, I made jewellery any time I could. Talking on the phone, watching TV, and long car rides became my production time. One night while watching a show with my family, I noticed something: all of *their* ten fingers. I gave my mom, dad, and Chandler strict instructions for making hemp jewellery and they became my labour force. I sold back more pieces than I could ever have done on my own.

LESSONS LEARNED

• Always ask for what you want and follow your vision. And, if you have an entrepreneurial spirit, even when it's scary or difficult, it's always more exhilarating and freeing to take risks and pursue opportunities than it is to work for someone else's vision.

Booty Beltz and Make It

I started my first "big girl" company, Booty Beltz, in 2003 as a project for a marketing class at the University of Alberta. A Booty Belt is a simple scarf belt onto which a buckle is fastened so that the belt is easy to take on and off. At the time, it was a pretty trendy look! After completing a business plan for the product, I was so full of passion and excitement that, after graduation, I threw caution to the wind and give the idea a go.

At first, I humbly went store to store with my bag of Booty Beltz and showed any store buyer who would give me a couple minutes of their time. Soon, after saturating the Edmonton market, I took business trips to Calgary, Montreal, Toronto, and Vancouver. After about a year, Booty Beltz were being sold in more than 30 stores across the country. I was 24 years old and had massive dreams of building a Booty empire. I signed up for the largest apparel show in the world, the MAGIC tradeshow in Las Vegas. It cost about $10,000, but despite the huge investment, something told me that it was the right move. So off I went, with Chandler to help me out, a suitcase full of Booty Beltz, and big dreams of world domination.

The first two days of MAGIC were grim, without a single order placed. On the third day, a couple of small orders trickled in, but nothing close to what I had imagined. On the final day of MAGIC, I spent most of it moping (a dangerous state to be in while in Vegas), but young Chandler worked a bit of his own magic and a department store from Japan ended up placing an order for 60 locations.

This was a total game changer, and I quickly upped my production crew of a few stay-at-home moms to a small factory in Edmonton. Preparing the order was exhilarating but also a ton of work and stress. It forced me to get organized quickly so that I'd be ready when another order of its size rolled in.

Unfortunately, trends changed, and when Booty Beltz was no longer on trend, orders blew through like tumbleweeds. Then, out of the blue, I was invited to split a booth at an art festival in downtown Edmonton to sell off some excess inventory. I didn't know if selling direct to consumers would be good for my "prestigious" Booty Beltz brand, but it sounded like fun, so I said yes. To my surprise, what I experienced changed the course of my business and my life. I thoroughly enjoyed selling directly to the people who would be wearing my belts instead of to intermediaries who didn't seem to care about them all that much. It *was* fun, and exciting, and I loved leaving the festival with pockets full of cash!

This inspired me to start setting up booths at craft fairs, musical festivals, and any other event that would have me. I began travelling all over the country with Booty Beltz and moved more product than I had when the belts were selling in more than 120 stores. I also connected with countless amazing artists, crafters, and makers from across Canada.

In the mid-2000s craft fairs weren't seen as the hip, cool events they are today. I could see, however, a strong resurgence of the handmade, DIY culture as Etsy started to gain momentum. What would happen, I wondered, if craft fairs were given a marketing makeover so that people my age would want to attend? A few months later, a friend and I launched our first show, complete with live music and a bar.

Within a year, the show grew from 25 exhibitors to well over 100. Seeing this massive growth made me want to expand to other cities. My business partner felt differently, so we decided to part ways. But Chandler had always taken a keen interest in my activities and he had launched his own T-shirt company, Ole Originals, because he wanted to cater to the bored dudes who were being dragged to craft fairs. He quickly had a monopoly and even quit his full-time marketing job to pursue his new venture. My brother and I joined forces and launched Make It in 2008.

Our first event in Vancouver was at the Roundhouse Community Centre, but we moved to a larger venue, the Croatian Cultural Centre, for the next three years. In 2013, we took a big leap of faith and moved to the PNE Forum, a 45,000-square-foot space in which we were able to accommodate 250 "Makies" (what we lovingly call our exhibitors). The show was a huge success and attracted over 15,000 Vancouverites.

In 2016, a large Toronto-based company approached us because it wanted to buy Make It. However, after six months of negotiation, in the final days of closing the deal, I had a sudden change of heart. Chandler didn't feel the same way, though, and was ready to close. Our only solution was for me to buy him out of Make It, which I did in the winter of 2016. There were lots of bittersweet emotions, but I know in my heart that it was the right move for both of us. Chandler still runs Ole Originals, which has grown into a very successful clothing brand.

As for me, I feel more passionate and excited about Make It than ever before. In 2015 we moved to the Edmonton Expo Centre which was a massive increase in size from our former venue. We also launched a new spring show at the PNE Forum in 2016, and in 2017 we relaunched in Calgary for spring and holiday shows. This expansion was really scary because there was so much uncertainty but I kept thinking about how many Makies I would be able to serve and how excited all the shoppers would be to see them.

LESSONS LEARNED

- An entire journey can stem from a little idea that you decide to take seriously. Always having the attitude that anything is possible allows things to happen. With entrepreneurship on the rise, especially for women, it's important to remember that fact. You just have to decide you're going to make it happen!

Make It Happen

For a long time, I wanted to write a book because my journey and experience that has come full circle has given me lots to share. So, finally, I decided to get serious and commit to finishing it. It was yet another make it happen journey.

Writing a book was a lot more work than I had anticipated and many times I wanted to quit. Brainstorming ideas, interviewing fascinating people, and sharing information are aspects that I loved. But there were less-than-fun times when the writing didn't flow. I have a lot of energy, so sitting in front of a computer for hours on end can be downright painful... especially on a warm, sunny day!

There was also editing, during which I sent everything I created to someone who pointed out all the improvements that could be made and questioned some of my ideas. Plus, putting a book on the market opens me up to potential criticism and scrutiny. But if I had quit, a part of me always would have wondered what could have been, so despite the many justifiable reasons for quitting, I stuck with it and made it happen.

LESSONS LEARNED

• Sometimes you have to give it everything you've got to cross the finish line and rejoice in the feeling of completing a project—for the sole reason that you wanted to do it *and* you did it. Completion is so much more satisfying when the stakes are high and you've invested yourself fully.

Adventures Await

I'm fortunate to be in a place in my life where I feel a sense of establishment. The year 2018 marked the tenth anniversary for Make It. My entrepreneurial journey has come full circle in many ways: I began selling my own line at very small craft fairs, and now I organize one of the largest fairs in the country. Writing this book has allowed me some beautiful reflection on my own journey—I stop and do that not nearly enough, which is probably true for you too. As creative entrepreneurs, we're forward thinking and moving, and sometimes it's easy to forget to stand still for a few moments and look back at how far we've come.

My hope is that this book provides you with the tools you need to fulfil your entrepreneurial dreams. When one person manifests their ideas in the world, we all benefit. Creation is a natural human ability, and with all the distractions that we go to when we're tuning out, it's important to remember what our inherent nature is. You were born for greatness, just like every other living being on this planet. You were put here to shine brightly and do great things. The only thing that might be getting in your way, ironically, is you. How crazy is that?

Make It Real

Reflect on your own life. There is so much wisdom and richness in where we've been, which helps us get to where we want to go.

1. In your journal, write about your early entrepreneurial experiences. When you were a child, did you have your own business, for example, a lemonade stand or a bike wash? What was it like? How did you feel about it? These glimpses of early entrepreneurship are sure signs of what's to come. Not everyone is wired the same way and there's a reason that you've been drawn to starting a business.

2. Review what you've written and note what special qualities or gifts showed up in your early endeavours. Take a few moments to acknowledge and appreciate these gifts. They are in you forever and very precious, even if you've forgotten about them or haven't tapped into them for a while.

three

Making It on Your Own

· ·

"Infuse your life with action. Don't wait for it to
happen. Make it happen. Make your own future.
Make your own hope. Make your own love.
And whatever your beliefs, honor your creator,
not by passively waiting for grace to come
down from upon high, but by doing what you
can to make grace happen... yourself, right
now, right down here on Earth."

BRADLEY WHITFORD

THERE'S NO MAGICAL universal formula for making it
happen. I'm sorry to disappoint you if you thought I
was going to give you the key to creating your dream
life. There are a ton of books, workshops, and online courses
that claim they have the secret solution that will make all the
difference. If someone says they have all the answers, run!
They're probably in it to make a quick buck by preying on
people's vulnerabilities.

Each of us has a unique "make it happen equation" based on our personalities, characteristics, and experiences. This equation is as individual as fingerprints. What motivates and inspires us to succeed is different for you than it is for me. There are commonalities that we'll explore, but you've got to create and manifest what you desire in your life using your own formula by first discovering the elements that best suit you. Think of "making it" as your own special mathematical equation.

To explain how this works, I'll share with you my own magical making it happen formula:

My Why + Focus + Environment + Team + Accountability + Self-Care + Fun = It Happening

My Why

The first aspect of this equation is "my why," which refers to inspiration, clarity, and drive. The *reason* anyone does something is the driving force behind creation. If the why behind your actions isn't strong, there won't be enough momentum. While every formula is unique, knowing your purpose is key to making it happen. When you know your why and act accordingly, like an airplane, you'll experience a critical moment when you go from rolling down the runway to liftoff. If there isn't a compelling reason to do something significant, you'll likely spin your wheels for a long time before you get anywhere.

My why for the Make It show is creating a platform for Makies to be able to earn a living doing what they love. I know first-hand how amazing that feels, and I want to help others to experience it too. There are other legitimate reasons that I do what I do, but they have not nearly as much weight.

Focus

When you're a creative person, it's easy to be distracted by shiny objects. Focus, therefore, is a key element in my make it happen equation. There have been many times when my eyes have been larger than my stomach and I've piled up my plate with a ton of exciting projects, thinking I'll get around to doing them all. The truth is, the more I have going on, the less likely it is I'll be able to complete anything fully.

When you focus your attention on something, it's truly amazing how it transforms and takes shape. For me, there is so much comfort and satisfaction in having substantial chunks of time to devote to something I'm passionate about creating. When my energy and intention become focused like a laser beam, there's nothing I can't do. That doesn't mean it's going to be easy, but it's a more intentional, direct process that saves time and energy.

Environment

My next factor is environment. I'm a feelings-based person, sensitive to light, sounds, touch, energy, and just about everything else. So, to create, I have to be comfortable. I try not to be a total pain in the ass (PITA), but if I'm given a hotel room, a table in a restaurant, or something else that doesn't feel right, I politely ask for a switch. Sometimes the people I'm with think I'm being difficult and other times they're thrilled I took the initiative. When you ask for things nicely, it's amazing how helpful others can be.

When I'm in a creative flow, my surroundings are even more important. While writing this book, I had to make sure my kitchen table/office felt inspiring and cozy. I always have candles and incense burning, along with a cup of tea and soothing beats. If I feel relaxed and content, my writing flows so much better.

Team

Another important factor in my equation is my team. I have to work with people who I admire and respect. If I don't click with someone, I can't move forward. I've learned that, in this respect, being a PITA is a very good thing. So much energy gets wasted when you work with clashing personalities that just don't fit. The Make It team is a tight-knit crew of co-workers and friends who work hard together to pull off the shows, and we also love to share stories and bond over a glass of wine. Going to work is fun and as a result we get the job done with smiles on our faces (most of the time)!

It's incredible what a group of people who share a like-minded why can pull off. At the beginning of my journey, and for many years it was a solo pursuit. Finding people who shared my vision and saw what I wanted to do took time, and it was surreal when it finally happened.

Accountability

Somewhere along the line, there needs to be accountability so that I commit to finishing. Otherwise I might as well buy a one-way ticket to Procrastinationville! The formula for producing Make It has tremendous accountability baked right into the business model. We set the show dates and locations years in advance, and each year we have to produce shows to a high level on those days in those cities. No ifs, ands, or buts. Those hard deadlines ensure Make It keeps happening.

Through the show, I'm accountable to the Makies and shoppers. I'm also accountable to other people who resonate with my message. I feel a personal obligation to share what I've learned with those who can benefit from it. My story is varied and based on all levels of the handmade world. But I've also learned from the stories that have been shared with me in the many conversations I've had with artists and makers over the years. I picked up on behavioural patterns of creative entrepreneurs by listening and observing and reflecting within. My goal with this book is to share all this intel with you so that you don't have to make some common mistakes because you will have a deeper awareness.

Self-Care

Self-care is something that drives me insane! I know how important it is, and yet I often feel so resistant to it. I've nose-dived into burnout more than a few times. I tell myself I'll never do it again, but something about minor self-sabotage feels sickly good. In the book *The Big Leap*, Gay Hendricks calls this "upper limiting." When things start to feel too good, it's tempting to take yourself down a notch by not loving yourself enough.

It's a misunderstanding to think that self-care is all about bubble baths, massages, and pedicures. It goes much deeper than that. Self-care is about doing the most nurturing thing for yourself as often as possible. This doesn't mean that you don't push yourself to achieve, but there's a gentleness that acts as a sweet counterbalance. Self-care means loosening the grip and doing what feels most empowering for you in every given moment. Be easy on yourself but continue to hold the vision tight.

My own self-care includes moving my body as often as I can and putting good things into it. I'm not an extremely health-conscious person, but I do know that having a base-line standard for how you take care of your body is crucial. If you don't, it will start to break down little by little. I also meditate and regularly share my feelings with close friends. Emotional and spiritual self-care is just as important as physical.

Fun

Having fun is everything to me! If what I'm doing doesn't feel enjoyable, then I don't really want to do it. However, something must be made very clear: there will be days that don't feel fun at all. In fact, they will suck. Things that are unexpected and negative will happen. The key is to see these in the most positive light you can. In the moment, this might be impossible, but keep going because better days are just around the corner.

We make our own fun. I was once at an employment law session at an entrepreneurial conference in Vancouver. You might think this sounds like a rather dull subject, but the presenter was funny and animated and she totally stole the show. She made employment law fun!

At Make It we've consistently focused on making it fun. From morning high-fives before the show opens to Makie events to wine nights with the team, I've purposely infused fun into the business because that's what has always been a huge driver for me. Life is short, so you might as well enjoy it.

Discover Your Formula

You are extremely special. Creative entrepreneurs are a rare, beautiful breed of risk takers who are willing to put it all on the line in pursuit of their true gifts. Magic happens when people are devoted to giving their all to what they believe in.

- Dig deeply into your own self to discover *why* you want to realize your dreams.

- Then put the other factors of your unique formula into place to manifest your vision.

You've got to see yourself for the spectacular human being that you are, follow that unique expression of creativity within you, and let it inspire you.

When you dream of making big things happen in your life, you lose yourself in time and space. There's a feeling inside that you can't deny or ignore. You know about all the reasons why your idea might not work out, but a little voice tells you to keep going—no matter what. This voice knows what you're capable of and pushes you to carry on even when you don't think that you have anything left in you to give. It knows that, although it's not always easy, it's what you're meant to do and the feeling of not doing it is worse than the fear that you might not succeed. You were born to do this and everything you need is already inside you. No one can take that away. Making it happen looks different for everyone, but when you're in this mindset, you'll be driven to make your vision a reality.

Your formula will become apparent as you look at the patterns in your own behaviour. When you reflect on your accomplishments, consider what factors determined your ability to focus on them through to the end. Your formula could be similar to mine or completely different. The way you get from conception to final product can look different from project to project. No pathway through the woods is exactly the same, just like no make it happen journey copies another exactly.

Make It Before You're Ready

Even with your formula in place, it's important that you *don't* have all the answers before you start. You might have an idea about marketing and selling your art or growing your business to the next level or something else, and that's great. But the true secret to making it happen is that you've got to shift how you perceive the world and change what you think. To start this journey, you don't need to have all your ducks in a row. Not even close. You don't have to label what you're doing or know exactly what it looks like. You just need to take the first steps toward something and the Universe will meet you halfway.

Consider this: could the you of 5, 10, or 20 years ago have imagined all the twists and turns of experience that have led you to the place you are today? Have you always known, while you were having them, what your experiences were adding up to? It's only when I look back on my story that I can make sense of the trail of breadcrumbs that led me from this experience to that. Little moments and decisions that sometimes feel insignificant when we make them shape our paths and allow our journeys to unfold. It's by answering our calling every day that things begin to shift.

Making it happen isn't about having a laser-focused plan or being overly controlled or disciplined. It's about following the little impulses along the way. Then, by fully trusting and surrendering, the process becomes less about you. When my business partner Ally and I started our first craft fair in 2007, we had no idea what we were signing up for. I wouldn't have guessed that the little fair we created without much of a plan would evolve into one of the largest craft shows in Canada. We just heard the call to do our event, and we answered it. Then we paid attention to our curiosity and dedicated ourselves to taking risks and finishing what we started.

Serving Others

Making it happen is also about showing up to serve other people. This book has my name on it, but it was written because I had open conversations, asked deep questions, and listened closely for the answers. I took polls on social media to find out what people struggled with so that I could research their issues and how to solve them. Creating this book was a collective effort. A lot of art is too, whether you're creating with other people or with a spiritual presence.

For instance, let's consider Andrew Lloyd Webber. In the summer of 2017, I saw *The Phantom of the Opera* again, this time with one of my best friends. We discovered that we had both seen the same production in Edmonton about 25 years ago, long before we knew each another. That performance rocked my 12-year-old soul and inspired something deep inside me. My friend had a similar experience, and it was magical to see the show with her as an adult.

Although I didn't completely understand the story of *Phantom* when I was a kid, it called me to the stage, and for a very long time, my biggest passion was performance art.

I dreamed of moving to New York City to study theatre. Even though I didn't end up becoming a professional performing artist, my love for the arts has brought me a lot of joy.

I wonder, though, if I hadn't seen *Phantom* when I was young, would I have developed such passion for the performing arts? Perhaps I would have seen something else later on and been equally moved. But I imagine the world would be different if Andrew Lloyd Webber hadn't made it happen, touching so many people's lives because he did. People in the handmade community might think the same thing about the Make It shows, and those who are served by your vision might feel the same way about you.

CASE STUDY
Dan Emery of East Van Light
(eastvanlight.com)

Dan has been participating in Make It since 2016, but he's so involved in the community, it's easy to forget that he hasn't been there from the start. His company is called East Van Light, and Dan, himself, is also a bright light. Whenever I see him at the show, he's always smiling and genuinely looks happy to be in his booth. You can tell he loves what he does and his product is a reflection of that. It was literally a "light bulb moment" that led Dan to start his unique company producing handcrafted, industrial lamps.

Growing up in Montreal, Dan had a ton of energy. One day, he and his friend Mark came up with the entrepreneurial idea to rake their neighbours' leaves. Since they were about seven years old, they didn't know what to charge and decided on the low price of 25 cents a bag. Even though this was back in the '80s, they soon learned that they were seriously undercharging. But because of the low price, every neighbour on the street was requesting their services.

As Dan and Mark grew older, they expanded their business into producing magic shows. In fact, they used some of the money they earned by raking leaves to buy tricks at the magic store. Soon, clients began hiring these young men to perform at their children's birthday parties. And, since they were now 12 years old, they knew their value and charged a respectable $25 per hour-long show. Parents loved the service, and Dan and Mark offered it until they were in high school. There were times when they wanted to charge more, but the idea always made them nervous.

At Concordia University, Dan studied communications and had a passion for music, which he explored all aspects of, including playing, producing, and promoting. For his less savvy friends, Dan started a small record label so that he could help them book gigs and tour. He did this for three or four years, but it wasn't something that he envisioned doing as a career because it didn't bring in much money. His passion was for the music and helping his friends succeed.

What Dan loved most about music was getting people engaged and excited. He knew that when they listened to music it evoked positive emotions and brought them to beautiful places. Things got dicey at times, particularly when there was poor communication between him and his friends. Apparently, young dudes aren't the best communicators. But Dan constantly asked himself what he wanted to do, how he could do it better, and how he could add value. He was somewhat successful in the music business because he could think like both an entrepreneur and an artist, which is a rare hybrid.

Once graduated, to pay the bills, Dan got a steady job with the film board. He wanted to keep music as a side hustle because he didn't want to compromise his creativity to make money. This freed him from too much worry and allowed him to enjoy his creative pursuits for what they were. Because of his boundless energy, he was willing to work all the time. He also didn't value his time as much as he does now.

While still in Montreal, Dan and his girlfriend at the time began flipping houses. With so much at stake, the business was addictive. He had to learn about construction, including how to electrically wire a house. According to Dan, they were so young that they didn't fully understand all the difficulties that could arise and the consequences. If he had known how much work it was going to be, he wouldn't have started to begin with.

Dan and his girlfriend finally decided that one of their houses would be their last, that once they completed the renovations they would move in and start a new chapter of their lives. But his girlfriend got a job in Vancouver, so they never moved in. Right before they relocated, a friend that knew about Dan's love of old things gave him a vintage light bulb because he thought it would look cool incorporated into the house. That fateful day, as Dan held the light bulb in one hand and a piece of wood in the other, he had an idea that would change his life.

Dan went to the hardware store and bought the parts he needed to attach the bulb to the piece of wood. With some tinkering, he created the first official East Van Light, which he still uses in his office as a reminder of how far he has come. The day he made it, Dan could not have guessed that his creation would become a prototype for a business that, within a few years, he would do full time.

After creating a few rudimentary lights, Dan moved to Vancouver. As the designs improved, he began to post photos of them on Facebook to show his friends. He was delighted when they not only liked the lights but wanted them for themselves. Because Dan wasn't a highly skilled carpenter, he sought out someone to help him source walnut and shape it into attractive stands that he would wire for the vintage light. Because he was making a more refined product, quicker, he was ready for his first craft fair.

With a Google search, he found a well-known craft fair in Vancouver, noticed the deadline was a couple days away, applied, and to his surprise got in. He started with about 70 lights in stock and by the end of the weekend he had less than 20. For his first show, it felt like a huge success and Dan was hooked on craft fairs.

One of the things Dan loved most about Vancouver was the tight-knit maker community. He felt supported from day one and at shows he met people who became very close friends. Dan's first Make It, in 2016, was the biggest show he'd done yet and he recorded his highest sales to date.

Dan has struggled with learning how to price his product properly. In the beginning, the lamps were *way* too cheap and he hardly made any money, but because of the low price, he sold a lot of them and built a loyal fan base. Now, he's better able to create a price structure that works, but he still struggles with finding the sweet spot. He's not alone in this. I see other Makies dealing with similar issues. It's so hard to know what to charge for your time when you're doing what you love and it doesn't actually feel like work.

Dan never set out to form a business. His story is a series of serendipitous events that allowed something he was passionate about to evolve into a living. He learned to follow his curiosity and trust his gut. East Van Light is a combination of all the things he loved most about construction with none of the headaches of flipping houses.

Dan recently left a job at TELUS to run East Van Light full time. He has been in business for only a few short years but has been hand-picked to participate in big shows across North America. The future is *so* bright for Dan and I'm stoked to see what he does next. He's made so much happen in such a short time, and it's just the beginning.

Here are Dan's best tips for making it happen:

- Give yourself a reality check occasionally and take responsibility for where you're at now and where you want to go.

- Shed everything that doesn't provide value and meaning in life. Only do things that bring a sense of fulfilment.

- Do fewer things better and surround yourself with people who support you.

- Fall in love with finishing.

- Talk to other people in your community because everyone struggles with similar things and can offer one another so much support.

- Believe it in your gut and your heart will tell you the next steps.

- Try stuff and listen to the reactions from customers.

- Use excitement as the fuel that propels you forward.

- Remember that, if you're at a show and it's not going well, it's just a moment in time. You never know what might happen, so you have to keep smiling—and stay off your phone.

Making It on Your Own

As creative entrepreneurs, we often feel truly alone. There's nothing else like desiring to make it happen—especially when you have a big dream that you so desperately want to manifest. You see it in such clear colour and know that special spark is within you.

The hardest part about being an entrepreneur, and the reason so many shy away from it, is the stamina it requires to hold that vision clearly in your mind and know you will pursue it—no matter what. Your friends and family try to understand what you're going through, but it can be really difficult for them. Unless they've walked the walk, it's almost impossible for them to know the highs and lows you go through. When you're a creative entrepreneur making it happen, you will experience a fuller spectrum of emotions than most people feel. It's just what you sign up for when you say yes to your calling.

Many people live their lives lost in a world of conformity, doing what they think people expect from them. They let their dreams die a slow death, and their explanations about why are usually so valid and compelling that no one questions them. They let their boldness slip through the cracks, later to be shared in stories of what could have or should have been. Nothing is sadder than regret.

The crazy thing is, people will fight hard for their pain. You might have met people who desperately want to make something happen, but they've built such a wall of excuses to hide behind that they have no choice but to believe them. When you ask these people why they're not doing what they're passionate about, they argue with conviction in favour of their limitations.

That you are reading this now means you're not someone settling for a life of complacency. Even if you feel stuck or are just starting out on your journey and still discovering your true gifts, you have reason for celebration. You poked your head out from under the sand and are curious to see your reality differently. There's so much divinity in curiosity.

We are all born with creativity and curiosity flowing through us. But as we age, we are taught to be cautious and conform. Bills need to be paid and responsibilities met. Following a dream is childish and impractical. Then, sooner or later, we look back and wonder what the heck happened to the life we once imagined. It can seem so far from our current reality that we can't believe we ever dreamed so boldly.

Having It All

There's a lot of truth to the saying, "You can have it all, just not all at the same time." You *can* have it all, but you have to prioritize the most important things. Setting priorities can allow us to relax into the flow of life, understanding that we don't have to make everything happen all at once. If you did manifest everything you wanted all at the same time, it would be far too overwhelming! Surrendering to the fact that everything you want is already a possibility lets you trust that it's only a matter of time until it materializes.

Our brains are so powerful that our beliefs can manifest anything.

You are
limitless
in your
ability
to create.
. . . .

PLEASE REREAD the sentence on the previous page until you fully believe it. A lot of people don't fully understand how powerful they are. They might have had glimpses of their potential, but often the full force of their creativity hasn't been realized. Not every idea needs to be executed, and only you can determine which goals are worthy to pursue. Keep this in mind: no one's life is supposed to look like another's. If you compare yourself to others, you'll drive yourself crazy and will always be looking left and right instead of forward. The most successful people in the world got to where they are because they focused on their own path.

I've always loved the saying "fortune favours the bold." Boldness is an expression of the commitment to beliefs that allows magic to transcend. As creative entrepreneurs, we need to stake out what we want and commit to taking action to get there. Ask for what you want because if you don't, you'll never know what the answer could be.

Witnessing people committed to their dreams delights me. Some people may want you to cave in or give up because that would justify their own beliefs and limitations. This is why it's imperative to stay true to yourself and not discuss what you want with people who may desire for you to stay small. These aren't bad people; they just have a stronger human need for certainty. When you rise above the persona they project onto you, things can get funky and challenging for them. They don't mean for it to be like this, but there's a hard-wired safety mechanism in our DNA, and some people are ruled by it. (We'll talk about this more in chapter 7.)

Seeing Gifts in Everything

When you begin to see the gifts in everything and everyone, magic starts to unfold. The gems in our experiences are not always obvious—some of the best gifts are those that force us to look at ourselves, the people around us, or a situation with greater clarity. Mirrors can be scary when the reflection isn't what you recognize or expect. In my own experience, when you understand that everything life hands you is a lesson or opportunity to learn, miraculous results occur. You will see how life is happening *for* you instead of *to* you. Realizing that there's a force in the Universe collaborating with you allows everything to shift and an awakening occurs.

This is a very exciting time to be alive. Change is happening all around us and exponential growth is possible. People are open to talking about consciousness like they never were before. Gone are the days when spirituality was a taboo topic. Now it's commonplace to talk about miracles, magic, and divine intervention. Hands up for self-actualization!

I've had several moments of divine intervention in my businesses, and they haven't all been blissful. Sometimes the lessons felt horribly unfair and difficult, but when I look back on them from a distance, I see the blessings and why I needed them. For instance, when you get to a certain level of business success, some people want to take you down. If you don't look for the gift in such an experience, it can feel sick, twisted, and messed up. But we're not to blame for other people's bad behaviour. Hurt people hurt and free people free.

When you believe that there's love in the teaching of every experience, you can see things differently. This is a huge work in progress for me and many times when something seemingly unjustified happens, I feel devastated, like a victim, and that life is unfair. But knowing that we're free and allowing others to be free too lets us release the negative energy. It doesn't belong to us.

I encourage you to practise your lessons too, interpreting whatever you experience in life as happening for your benefit in some way. Remember, life is happening *for* you not *to* you. You can relax into the moment, knowing that whatever happens is exactly what's meant to be. Even the most challenging moments pass eventually.

Creation and Manifestation

Making anything remarkable happen requires a whole lot of work, but it's really true that when we do what we love for a living, we never work again. Sure, not everything is fun, but with the bigger picture in mind, resistance to doing all the little things to get where we need to go falls away. We can see the bigger picture, knowing with certainty it's serving a greater good.

Take writing this book. In the beginning, it was easy because I just plunked down in front of my computer every day and let thoughts pour out of me, savouring the sensation of channelling information through my fingers. But when I decided I wanted to create a "real book," I had to set some parameters and felt a lot of resistance, which I didn't enjoy at all. It meant facing hard realities about who I was and what I was made of. But then a pivotal moment of grace occurred and I began applying to my life all that I had been learning from my research. Submerging myself in the subject of manifestation, I felt my own brain changing.

To be completely transparent and vulnerable with you, there were many days when I felt so scared about what people would think about this book that I almost stopped in my tracks. I am mostly a confident person, but my resistance to completing the project was on a whole new level. To an extent, I can hide behind the Make It brand, but the idea of publishing a book with my name on it brought on anxiety and dread. To make it happen, I had to face these aspects of myself while still forging ahead.

Creative entrepreneurship is an art form that embodies the same processes of creation as any other artistic pursuit. There's the vision, the process, and the manifestation, and you never know exactly what you're going to make until you've made it. This is why it's never worth the time and energy to worry about competition because no one else can create something exactly like you can, and you can't create something just like anyone else. Your competitor can only do what you've already done, not what you'll do next.

When you fully embrace who you are as a unique medium of creation, you'll be vibing at a higher level and understanding things you simply couldn't before. The reason why things that seemed unfair or wrong happened will start to shift into focus and become increasingly clear. You'll see lessons in all your endeavours. When life starts to feel this way, you'll know you're in the miraculous sweet spot of manifestation.

Make It Real

Get to know better your own formula for making it happen by doing the following:

1. In your journal, write about why you want to make it happen. Who does your idea serve and how can it help? When you have clarity about who will benefit from what you make, everything gets easier and becomes more real.

2. Write without censoring your thoughts. Allow a stream of consciousness to explore your limiting beliefs and all the compelling reasons for fighting the limitations that hold you back. Don't edit. Just let the pen flow across the page. Most importantly, don't judge yourself.

3. Review your limiting beliefs one by one and challenge their validity. When you see how unfounded some of your limiting beliefs are, you may be able to let them go instantly. Some might trip you up and cause you to fight for your pain, and that's okay. You may not be ready to let that one go. But at least you're aware now and can make the shift in perception when you're ready.

4. Recall an experience from the past that felt hard or unfair. What was its gift? What did you learn from it and what have you carried forward that helps you in your life today? Explore this deeply so that you start to see the trail of breadcrumbs that brought you to this moment.

5. After exploring exercises 1 to 4, piece together your own make it happen equation. What are the key ingredients you need to move the needle, eventually complete a daunting project, and move up a level in your life? Are there patterns in your formula, or does it depend on what you're trying to achieve? The more you write the more clarity you'll achieve.

Part Two

. . . .

MAKING
IT
HAPPEN

four

Knowing What "It" Is: Turning Your Light On and Letting It Shine

"You can't just sit there and wait for people to give you that golden dream. You've got to get out there and make it happen for yourself."

DIANA ROSS

HAVING AN INNER spark that inspires us to take this wild ride as creative entrepreneurs is a quality we all share. Knowing this, it's time to clarify what to do next. What exactly do you want to make happen? What's your inner calling spurring you on to do right now? Where do you want to be in 1 year, 5 years, or 10 years, or any time in between? When you're clear about who you are, what you've done, and where you want to go, doors, windows, skylights, and all sorts of things open for you! You're attracted to the idea of making it happen for a reason. I'm going to ask you to clarify what you want to make happen. But first, we need to know what *it* is.

Collaborating with the Universe

The life we live today is made up of countless decisions and patterns we've cultivated along the way. If you're reading this now, it means you've heard the call to level up and take a leap of faith to something even bigger. That is so exciting and I couldn't be more thrilled for you. Life gets way more fascinating when you go where the Universe gently (or sometimes aggressively) nudges you to expand.

There's no denying that a force greater than ourselves is at work, supporting us. You might want to call this God, spirit, energy, universal force, or something else. All these words are interchangeable. If you believe that you'll always be supported in what you do, then there are no bad choices to make. Crazy, right? What's even nuttier is the amount of time and effort we devote to worrying about things that we can't control. Letting go of this clenching need allows things to work out naturally, the way they're supposed to.

Make
"trust and
surrender"
your mantra
whenever you
feel fear.

· · · · · · · · · · · · · ·

"Trust and surrender" is a simple but incredibly challenging thing to do. As entrepreneurs, we do a lot of planning,
forecasting, and making decisions that aren't too risky—the
necessary stuff that, all too often, comes from using our
heads instead of our hearts. The heart operates within a
totally different system, and the wisdom you receive from it
might not even make sense at first.

For instance, I was meditating when I received a clear
message that I should travel across the world to Bali to focus
on finally making my book project a reality. In the past, I had
taken a few stabs at writing it but had never seen it through.
Somehow, I knew this time would be different. A strong
impulse told me that if I went to Bali I would receive what I
needed to write something that would serve my community.

When I searched for flights, I selected two random dates
in the fall. The price for the flight was an incredibly low $590.
I have spent much more than that to fly from Vancouver to
Toronto. I thought it must be a website glitch and played
around with different dates. But for whatever reason, the
dates I originally chose were hundreds of dollars cheaper
than at any other time. I tried my best not to overthink it
and booked my flight immediately.

When something feels easy, it means it's right.

I call this state of ease "flow," and it feels good because it's our natural state of being. Things work out and align in unexpected ways.

Unfortunately, many people are freaked out by flow, so as soon as things start to feel *too* good they self-sabotage to get back to a place that feels more comfortable. It's as though we were hard-wired to struggle so that when we feel a natural flow, it's uncomfortable, and sometimes we resist it. This is especially true if you're not used to something being easy—which most of us aren't. Life doesn't have to be hard. It can feel effortless and fun. This doesn't mean you won't have to work diligently or that you won't have difficulties, but life can radically improve if you allow flow to happen. Accept ease and grace as your default.

There's a force in the Universe that loves us so much that it wants us to be greater than we can comprehend. A next-level destiny awaits each of us, and the only requirement for reaching it is becoming more of who we authentically are.

Define Your Vision

When you're in the process of defining your vision, it's important to let the universal force in so that it can help guide you. Attuning to the frequency of the Universe is like tuning in to your favourite radio station. This is an old-school analogy, but there was a time when you had to subtly turn a dial, making small adjustments to get the clearest signal possible for listening to your favourite song. Similarly, we have to listen carefully to attune to the universal frequency, and the more aligned we are with it, the clearer the guidance is. We each have ways of adjusting our dial, and I encourage you to do at least one of these things every day:

- Meditate
- Go for a walk
- Spend time in nature
- Exercise
- Garden
- Do martial arts
- Dance
- Read inspirational books
- Have conversations with amazing people

Connecting every day with a higher vibration will make you more aware of its presence throughout the rest of your life and more attuned when it's clearly sending a message about your next move. I'll go into greater detail later on in the book.

Why Meditate?

Meditation allows us to quiet our chatterbox brain enough to hear the messages from deep within. I'm constantly asking questions about what to do next, and if I get quiet enough, I almost always hear my answers. Sometimes I don't understand them at first, but if I surrender and trust, they become clear. The trick is to slow down so that this wisdom can come forward. It usually speaks in subtle whispers, which is why so many people never really hear it. But if you ignore it for too long, it will become so loud that you'll be forced to pay attention. Disease and accidents are very common, direct ways in which the Universe communicates.

We are so wise, and everything we need to know is available to us. But we often miss the messages because they exist in the present moment, and we don't. We are so distracted, especially with all our beeping, flashing gadgets. Our brains love to mull over issues that happened in the past and over-analyze what might happen in the future. If you feel worries, stress, or as though you don't have control over the direction of your life, it might be it's because you aren't living in the present moment most of the time. People meditate because it's a deliberate practice of being in the moment.

Here is the only thing we have. Now. Now. Now. If you're an A-type personality who loves to plan and endlessly come up with ideas for the future, you might be thinking, *How can I do the necessary planning if I'm always thinking about now?* I, myself, have asked this question a lot.

We can shift our focus to whatever we're currently doing. We can choose to be present when we plan for the future, and when we're finished planning, we can then focus our consciousness on the next task at hand. Another word for this concept is mindfulness—maintaining an awareness of your thoughts and where your attention goes. If your thoughts drift, you make a conscious effort to bring them back to the present moment. Doing this repeatedly retrains your brain to behave. When we're fully present in this way, we usually do a better job—and generally faster and more efficiently too—than when we're distracted.

Multi-tasking has become normal for most of us. We eat our meals while checking Facebook and probably don't even taste our food as we chew. We do things then realize that we don't remember doing them. Nothing gets done well and we feel stressed and out of control. We become unconscious and can end up waking up in a place and wonder how the hell we got there.

The more you practise mindfulness, the more you'll consciously feel the experience of being in the flow. Things will feel effortless and you'll have the sensation that you're truly alive. When we are in flow, magic and miracles can be seen in everything—someone calls you seemingly out of the blue; you see something helpful that you hadn't noticed before; you have an experience of good luck.

Take Action

You have something extraordinary in you to give to the world. If you've been able to discover what this is already, you're very fortunate. Now it's important that you do everything in your power to actualize this expression to the highest level you can. When you're on the right path, things align to help you get exactly where you need to go.

If we know precisely what we want to do but don't know exactly how to start, it can be frustrating. At first, an idea may be really exciting, and we might spend time daydreaming about what it will be like when we carry it out. We might see ourselves as highly successful entrepreneurs who have achieved all the things we've always dreamed of and without a care in the world. It's fun to fantasize and most creative types are really good at it, spending a chunk of our lives with our heads in the clouds. It's doing the work to make our ideas a reality that's hard.

Taking the first steps might be easy. Let's take Anna, for example. She always loved photography and long dreamed of doing it professionally. She frequently thought about pursuing this path and shared her aspirations with her friends and family. Since they love her, they always encouraged her to make a go of it. She felt supported. So Anna researched the best equipment and bought all her gear. She was overjoyed and a little bit afraid because she had finally invested in her dream and it was becoming real. After bringing her new, shiny camera home, she set out to learn how it works. This was also thrilling, but a sense of panic grew inside her. She thought things like, *I hope I'll be able to figure out how to use all this expensive camera gear*, and, *Maybe I should have bought a cheaper model*. Her high gradually fell lower because doubt unfurled inside her, and it didn't feel good.

Suddenly, life was too busy and the demands of family, friends, and work became Anna's greatest concerns. She had the best intentions to start taking photos, but there just wasn't enough time in the day. Occasionally, she made moves toward the gear, but she needed to spend an entire day testing it out like she promised herself she would, and she couldn't find the time. Weeks rolled by and then months and then, the next thing she knew, it was Christmas and with all the festivities, she really did have zero time for herself.

Every once in a while, she looked at the camera sitting in the corner of her closet, gathering dust. She felt sad and regretful that she hadn't devoted time to pursuing what she once imagined might become her profession. It seemed like such a waste of money now, but Anna was also disappointed that she couldn't make it happen. She had found the first step of her goal easy, but the next step anything but.

If this story makes you cringe because you've experienced something similar, you are definitely not alone. There have been *many* situations in which I really wanted something but couldn't get through the resistance to get there. This is an awful feeling and very common for creatives. We dream big and it's a beautiful thing. We take the initial steps to go after our goals. But unless we're careful, we're too easily distracted.

Although I constantly battle with resistance, I've learned some helpful tricks that reset my course when I've drifted into the dangerous land of procrastination. Here are two important ones.

TIP 1: Build Your Awareness Muscle

The best thing you can do to overcome resistance is build your awareness muscle. As soon as you become aware that you've drifted from your goal, be blunt and honest with yourself in the same way a friend who you turn to for tough love would be. Sometimes you might hate it, but you know that she tells you the truth because, ultimately, she has your back. If you try on a dress while shopping with her, when you ask her how it looks, she's going to tell it to you straight whether you like the response or not. Honesty can be harsh if we aren't ready for it, but the truth sets us free.

For Anna, our wannabe photographer, plenty of times she told herself she would go out into nature to take photos for the day. But something always came up that prevented her from following through. This was undoubtedly frustrating, but if some honesty and discipline had been put into place, she could have avoided thwarting her own objective. When you're at work on your goals, take note of when you divert yourself from what you need to do to realize them. For example, do you:

- Turn to social media, mindlessly scrolling through posts for hours instead of learning that new program?

- Set aside time to work, but your friend calls and you wind up on the beach instead?

- Overschedule yourself and commit to things you know aren't all that important?

- Do non-priority tasks like cleaning out your sock drawer?

- Stay out too late or drink too much at a party when you know you need to get up the next morning and work?

- Show up late for an important meeting for no good reason?

- Take any other sneaky diversion that subverts your goal of making it happen?

Break the cycle by building the capacity to recognize how you get snagged.

Unconscious behaviour is composed of habits made by repeated action. If you can catch yourself doing it, you can change it. If you can deliberately interrupt an unwanted pattern, you can radically alter your life. The good news is, if you change one behaviour from negative to positive, it becomes easier to make more shifts in the right direction.

Tip 2: Set Your #1 Priority

We all have the same number of hours in the day, but it seems like some people are able to get *so* much more done. Why? Do they eat something special for breakfast?! What it comes down to is priorities. Remember, you can have it all, but you can't have it all at once. You must focus on the area you want to succeed in at a specific time, decide what you want to do, and determine how and when you're going to do it.

That sounds way too easy and simplistic, but that's really all it takes. For example, before I started writing this book, I talked about it a lot and knew in my heart I wanted to do it. But then I had to sit down and write something every day.

Many times, I've caught myself in the act of avoidance and procrastination. Social media is the *perfect* way to blow through large chunks of time without getting anything productive done. It's become so addictive that sometimes you don't realize you've been sucked in until it's too late and hours during which you could have been making it happen have slipped by. Because I wrote a big chunk of this book in Bali, I had an opportunity to completely unplug, and I was scared to do it. I was afraid that if I didn't have an escape, I would actually have to do the work. Knowing this gave me the freedom to break the habit.

Let Your Inner Light Shine

The closer I get to my inner light, the more it scares me. It feels so good but also so intense that it can seem overwhelmingly powerful. When I feel myself moving to a new level, I become nervous and sometimes terrified because it's an unknown to me. My human need for certainty flares up and I may self-sabotage to stay in a more comfortable place. But because I now have awareness of what the heck is going on, I can reset my thoughts and get back on track.

In an informal survey on Facebook, I asked my friends and Make It community what stops them from reaching their goals. The number one answer was fear of failure, followed by fear of success. Two outcomes that contradict each other scare us the most. The crux of it all is that discomfort and uncertainty can be terrifying. But safety and comfort are what mould us into mediocrity.

Another reason so many people are afraid to reach their goals relates to what it might mean to others. What will it be like if people think our creations suck? What will happen if people think that what we do is really, really good? Then what? Will things change? Will the people around us respond to us in the same way? If they don't, what does that mean?

The great spiritual teacher Marianne Williamson has shared many inspiring words of wisdom in her books. One of my favourite quotes of hers is from *A Return to Love*:

> Our deepest fear is not that we are inadequate. Our deepest fear is that we are powerful beyond measure. It is our light, not our darkness that most frightens us. We ask ourselves, Who am I to be brilliant, gorgeous, talented, fabulous? Actually, who are you *not* to be? You are a child of God. Your playing small does not serve the world. There is nothing enlightened about shrinking so that other people won't feel insecure around you. We are all meant to shine, as children do. We were born to make manifest the glory of God that is within us. It's not just in some of us; it's in everyone. And as we let our own light shine, we unconsciously give other people permission to do the same. As we are liberated from our own fear, our presence automatically liberates others.

When you make it happen, rising up and shining more light on the world is a priority. This is what you were put here to do. But when *it* actually happens, it comes with uncertainty and so can be uncomfortable. We don't feel in control of the situation and that's scary for our old lizard brain, which is designed to keep us safe and small. Expansion requires growth on many levels of your being—so no wonder it's awkward at times!

The next time you intend to do the work your inner voice is calling you to do, watch for peculiar sensations or thoughts that come to play. Without judging, notice what they say and what behaviours you engage that detract from the light you're meant to shine in the world. For instance, instead of working on the important task that deep down you know will take you to the next level, do you:

- Question yourself?
- Feel bored or antsy?
- Become a compulsive snack maker?
- Post something on every outlet of social media?
- Turn into a puppy interested in doing anything but sitting still?
- Do any number of other things to fritter away the time meant for you?

These little habits and distractions can be super-annoying, but it's possible to train our inner puppy just like we would a real one. Keep pulling your mind back to your priorities, reminding yourself that if you're serious about making it happen, at some point you must sit and stay with that scary, thrilling project that's going to propel you to the next level. But please don't be too hard on yourself either. It's so easy to feel like whatever we do isn't good enough or guilty about not doing what we said we would. Learn to loosen the grip a bit and allow things to ease up and flow.

Know What's Driving You

When you uncover *why* you distract yourself, so much magic is unveiled. The truth isn't always pleasant, but there is so much power in it. It's kind of like financial administrative work. For most creative folks, doing taxes and working on budgets can feel like a drag. But when we finally have no choice but to do them, we achieve a lot of awesome clarity. We can actually see what we're spending money on and how much we have.

When we stop distracting ourselves from our priority activities, the world opens up. But before that happens, we also have to build the muscle that allows us to switch gears. Dreams are easy but doing the work to realize them is hard because it requires discipline. That's why so many people fail to achieve what they desire. Simply put, everything you do either brings you closer to or further away from your desired result.

Let's take Jake, for example, and his goal to lose 20 pounds by summer. Maybe he sets his alarm for 6 a.m. so that he can get up early and go for a run, but when the buzzer goes off he feels too tired from his late night before, so he sleeps in and promises he'll run after work. After hitting the snooze button multiple times, he realizes that he no longer has time to make the green smoothie he planned and instead, on the way to work, he picks up a muffin that's guaranteed to be loaded with fat and sugar. By the time Jake gets to work, he already feels terrible about how the day started, so when a colleague invites him to lunch at a new burger joint, he figures he might as well. After work, his colleagues are having drinks to celebrate a birthday, and even though the run was a good idea, beer and wings sounds like more fun...

You can probably see that Jake will have a hell of a time losing 20 pounds by summer.

All the little day-to-day decisions you're making, probably without a lot of consciousness, paint the picture of your life.

Identify Your Desires

We need to know what we're going for and why because *when you see it, you can be it!*

Your desires are potent clues to discovering what will truly make you happy in life. For example, for as long as I can remember, I've had a deep desire for freedom. I've always known that I'm not cut out for the whole nine-to-five grind because I like to create my own schedule and fill it with things I want to do. I wrote these words in a stunning Airbnb in the Balinese jungle. At night, as I sat typing away at a gorgeous teak table, the buzz of crickets and frogs surrounded me. Floor-to-ceiling windows exposed a view of lush, thick vegetation. For me, the ability to set my own schedule and travel across the world to create this book for you is an expression of a deep desire. I have never been a fan of being told what to do and it feels amazing to have recognized that and to have made a life that I get to set the rules for.

When you think of your own desires, what comes up? Like me, do you crave autonomy, to be totally creative, or to give back to the community? Or maybe you love to feel stable and grounded or to have constant crazy adventures. Whatever your deep desires may be, it's a game changer when you identify them within you.

Clarifying your desires involves curiosity and having serious conversations with yourself. Probably not out loud in public, but quietly, gently within when you've set aside time to be introspective. To understand yourself better, you need to commit to spending more time alone, asking yourself questions and then carefully listening for the answers.

CASE STUDY
Sarah Mulder of Sarah Mulder Jewelry (sarahmulder.com)

Sarah Mulder has been participating at Make It since 2010 and has never missed a show. In the early days, when I also had a booth at the show, we were neighbours. We even did a trade and I still wear a necklace she made. Sarah is very positive and friendly and her mom, who often helps her in her booth, is the same way. Make It customers look forward to seeing them at every show.

As is a common theme, Sarah started her entrepreneurial journey at a young age. As a kid, she absolutely loved art and drew constantly. When Sarah's grandmother took care of her, she would give Sarah an entire roll of paper and by bedtime it would be completely filled with drawings. Drawing was all Sarah wanted to do, and she dreamed of being an art teacher when she grew up. Luckily, both her parents were very supportive of her love of art and made sure she always had ample supplies.

When she was the ripe old age of eight, Sarah started her first business selling—for 50 cents apiece, on the side of the road in East Vancouver—cards decorated with dandelions and other plants. Sarah says neighbours bought them because they felt sorry for her, but she didn't care because she was making money. While in junior high, she started painting images like Winnie-the-Pooh on T-shirts. The kids at school loved and wanted them too. Soon, she was back in business, painting shirts when she probably should have been doing homework. She sold them for about $20, which made for a nice profit in the late '90s.

For Sarah's 16th birthday, her mom bought a whole bunch of seed beads so that Sarah and her friends could make necklaces. That's when her love of jewellery making began. After creating a ton of necklaces, she signed up for some local craft fairs to sell her surplus stock. Her company was called Love, Sarah and she had a little stamp made to press on her tags. Now she was legit!

After high school, Sarah spent two years at Langara College, earning a fine arts degree. She then went to Europe for three months and learned art history, which was a big turning point because she experienced new cultures and saw the world outside her Vancouver bubble. When she returned, she attended Simon Fraser University but soon flunked out because her courses didn't interest her. She felt lost because all she wanted to do was travel. It wasn't until she enrolled in the fine arts program at Emily Carr University of Art + Design that things started to make sense.

She graduated in 2005, met her future husband at a party, and got a real job teaching art to elementary students. Things were on track, but it wasn't long before Sarah's entrepreneurial spirit felt neglected. Throughout this time, she had been occasionally selling jewellery at craft fairs but hadn't been doing much drawing or painting. When she came to Make It in 2010, she sold both her art and her jewellery but discovered that people were more interested in jewellery than in art, so she felt that was what she needed to focus on. And focus she did! Sarah created such a successful jewellery business that she quit her teaching job and never looked back. It was at her first Make It show that Sarah recognized her passion could bring in money.

But this didn't leave her any time to paint and she often missed it, although she needed to concentrate on her thriving jewellery business in order to pay the bills. Then, on a whim, she signed up for an abstract art class held by a prominent Vancouver painter. Taking that course changed the way she looked at painting and she became wildly passionate about creating art once again. Still, balancing her art creation with jewellery making continues to be a struggle.

In the beginning, Sarah spent money recklessly. Excited about her business, she forked out cash for tools and supplies before she was making anything with them. As a result, even today she has a lot of sample products that she doesn't know what to do with. Looking back, she regrets the purchases, but she's determined to repurpose and sell all the products she made with them so that she can recover each dollar that she originally spent.

Sarah continues to do Make It and many other shows, and she sells in about 20 stores across Western Canada. What I admire most about her is her constant commitment to upping her game. She collaborates with fashion designers and photographers to create stunning photo shoots with her jewellery. These not only look great to clients and wholesale accounts, but they give Sarah the ability to work with other creative minds that she so greatly admires.

Her philosophy for designing is to set trends rather than chase them. She'd rather create jewellery that speaks to people long term. Since she's so naturally outgoing, she loves to talk to customers at the shows and learn about what they want to wear. She creates jewellery that she loves because she knows it will resonate with her customers. Even though jewellery is a very competitive category, Sarah believes that there is enough to go around because customers are naturally attracted to different styles and designers. She also knows a big part of why she does so well at shows like Make It is because her booth looks professional and she and her mom have worked very hard to establish strong relationships with their loyal customers.

I'm always so excited to see how much Sarah up-levels from year to year. Her website, photos, and booth are so pro and inspire other Makies to up their game as well. The support of her family, friends, and customers keeps her business growing. Sarah feels that they believe in her so much that she has no choice but believe in herself too. Her philosophy is that creations are a collaborative process. It's such an honour to have Sarah as a Makie. Many of her peers look up to her as someone who continues to make it happen.

Here are Sarah's best tips for making it happen:

- Find out what products earn the most money so that you can make more of those.

- If you're confident about what you make, you don't have to worry about competition. Focus on what you're doing and that's it.

- Social media can be a big waste of time but it's a crucial marketing tool these days, so you have to learn how to use it without getting sucked in by it.

- Be consistent and aligned in everything you do. Your website, social media, and booth should look like they all belong to the same company.

- You have to love it. Know your audience and make them fall in love with what you're doing. Customers need you just as you need them, and they are taking a chance on you when they buy from you, so don't let them down.

- You need to self-reflect constantly. No one is going to tell you what to do next, so you must decide for yourself.

- If you want to get something done, you have to do it despite how scary or uncomfortable it might feel.

- When customers buy from you, they're taking a little part of you home with them. This is a special feeling that not a lot of people get to experience, so it's important to value it for the awesome thing it is.

Do the Work

Like Sarah, everyone I interviewed for this book said the secret to making it happen is that you just gotta do it. Nike was clever to use those three iconic words as its slogan because the saying is so simple but so true. If you want it to happen, you have to make it so.

But making it happen is a delicate balance of yin and yang. Working super-hard and getting shit done combines with softer, feminine energy that allows you to receive guidance and help. It's a dance between the two. You need to do the work and put in the time while allowing for something larger than yourself to guide you along the way. It's giving and receiving as you would in any other relationship.

Tony Robbins is a big-time action guy. I love how enthusiastic he is and the massive results I've been able to make in my own life by following his work. He's all about focusing on the outcome you want, getting into an optimal state, and then taking massive action immediately. There's no messing around when you follow Tony's formula, but he believes in allowing grace and gratitude to enter the equation too. Brute force isn't sustainable and there always needs to be a pull/push dynamic. This is true whether applied to making it happen with your body, business, closet, diet, or relationships.

Have you ever done something that ended up being super-challenging, but when you started out you had no idea about all the difficulties that were in store for you? If you had, you probably wouldn't have started on the path in the first place. I've felt this way *many* times, including while writing this book. It's taken a whole lot of time clacking away on the keyboard that I could have spent doing countless other activities. But until I got my butt in front of the computer, a book wasn't going to magically manifest. Any project you decide to make happen will require the process of putting one foot in front of the other, no matter how boring, repetitive, scary, or frustrating it might be. The sparkly, glamorous moments come later, but at the beginning it's about putting in the time and effort.

It can still be enjoyable and fun, but it takes consistent effort to move forward. I love Make It, but there are still some things on my list of tasks that I'd rather not do but must because they're necessary for the show and no one else can do them—like waking up at 6 a.m. on the morning of the opening to do a TV interview. It's already going to be a crazy-long day for me and I'd prefer more sleep, but press is vital for the show's success, so I'm happy to do it because it will result in a positive outcome.

Ultimately, doing the work is about tapping into the power that's within you. We are vessels for the Universe to use in the physical form, and to make it happen you have to allow yourself to open so the energy can flow through your body in an uninterrupted way. This is a big concept, but you'll get it when you see it in action.

Make It Real

To get into the flow, you have to commit to discovering and then practising what it feels like for you. The more flow you feel, the easier it will be for you to tap back into this frequency whenever you're pulled out of it. Anything worthwhile in life takes practice and discipline, but practising flow feels great, so you'll naturally want to stick with it.

1. Choose a manageable, fun morning practice. It could be going for a walk in nature, meditation, free-flow writing in your journal, or any other practice that makes you feel connected to a sense of something bigger than yourself. Commit to a week of it and notice any shifts. Next week, commit to another week of practice—the same one or a new one. And keep going. Describe the morning practice in your journal so you're clear about what it is and then schedule it as you would any other appointment.

2. Write a list of priority items to move you ahead. Once you have a complete list, rearrange it, ranking them in order of importance with the most important at the top. Start focusing your energy on completing the item at the top of your list until it's complete. Work through the rest of your list this way. Pick only one or two items to complete each day so you avoid overwhelming yourself.

3. On a large piece of paper, make a vision board (an image of the way you want your life to look). Start by choosing pictures, quotes, and words that call to you from magazines and/or other sources. Don't edit yourself or try to justify why you like the image, just cut. Choose

something to represent each of your desires. The images or words can be abstract but make sure you understand them and their significance to you. When you have something to represent each of your desires, arrange them on the paper so that the whole picture feels right to you. Only you will see it so don't worry whether it looks "cool." No art teacher will be grading this one. Let it speak to you in a multitude of ways. Make sure you feel inspired and happy when you look at your vision board. Put it up somewhere that you can see it as you make those dreams happen.

five

The "Make It Happen" Mindset: Thinking, Believing, and Doing to Make It Happen

"If someone else isn't making it happen for you,
make it happen yourself."

LAUREN MILLER

WHEN YOU'RE IN a "make it happen" frame of mind, you're in a groove or flow. You have a handle on what you think, and your thoughts are generally positive. When a negative thought comes up, you can see it for what it is and step away. You know that what you put out into the world is going to come back to you in one form or another. This is the basic idea behind the law of attraction. From choosing the energy we put into the world to making things easy for ourselves to being true to our authentic selves, the way we use our minds has a big impact on making it happen.

Choose Your Vibe

We can choose who we want to be in the world. This might make me sound a bit crazy, but I sometimes think of myself as two different people. There's Low Jenna and High Jenna. Often, I go on autopilot from one to the other, but if I remind myself to be conscious, I can take a step back and recognize who's steering the ship. I'll introduce you to my two different personalities, because I have a feeling you might have similar ones living in your head.

LOW JENNA:

- Is scared most of the time

- Feels like she's not doing enough

- Thinks people might not like her if she doesn't act a certain way

- Worries that people are out to get her

- Doesn't have certainty and that makes her feel insecure

- Is impatient and has the need to control situations so that they benefit her

- Isn't very trusting of others or herself

- Has a low energy and vibe

- Is competitive and wants to outdo others

- Fears she'll always be alone

- Worries that no one will give her the approval she needs in order to love herself

- Always wonders what's in it for her

- Doesn't feel secure or content in her body

- Thinks she should look a different way

- Judges others but is hardest on herself

- Believes it probably won't happen

HIGH JENNA:
- Is excited most of the time

- Thinks everything is awesome

- Is happy with her life

- Thinks people are there to support and love her

- Believes people want to see her succeed

- Knows there are many amazing opportunities for her to explore

- Has confidence that she can do whatever she puts her mind to

- Has as much fun as possible, every day

- Knows that everything meant to be will be

- Flows through life with grace and ease

- Loves everyone, including herself, and wants to see others succeed

- Is authentically herself no matter what the situation

- Feels that the Universe has her back

- Has an open mind and heart

- Has a sense of adventure and can't wait to explore

- Loves what she sees when she looks in the mirror

- Knows that with the right perspective every situation can be positive

- Believes with certainty and conviction it *will* happen!

Can you relate? Between these two Jennas, who would you want to bring to a party? Hopefully the second one!

You can choose who you want to be. Once you learn to control your mind, your life will start to miraculously shift. A miracle occurs when you can switch from low to high just like flicking on a light. Remember the analogy of tuning in to a radio station? You can home in on a signal that is clear and powerful.

Don't get me wrong. It takes a lot of work and discipline to be able to control our minds and it's rare for anyone to fully achieve this because so many of our beliefs are wired from the subconscious layers of our brains. You have programming that has been with you since you were a kid, and that doesn't dissolve instantly. But we can develop awareness through a daily practice of recognizing when we shift from high to low. The more you practise, the easier it will be. And the more comfortable you feel in a high place, the longer you'll be able to stay there.

A gifted homeopath offered me a visualization to help with shifting from low to high. She told me to picture myself in a hot-air balloon that was soaring upward. In order to go higher, I needed to release anything in the basket that wasn't serving me. Instead of feeling bad or guilty, I needed to trust that whatever I threw lovingly out of my basket would be nourished when it reached the ground below. When you catch yourself in that low place, try visualizing yourself in your own hot-air balloon, letting the negative thoughts fall to the ground as you float up.

Becoming truly happy can feel foreign, especially if you've spent a length of time in a lower vibration. It can be difficult to handle the high-vibe sensations and then it's tempting to sabotage your way back to a more comfortable place. Resist this urge with everything you have! You deserve to feel amazing and to have a fantastic life. When you are in a high place, things just start to work themselves out in your favour without a whole lot of effort. This is what it means to be in alignment.

You Become What You Believe

A strong belief in what I create has been a major factor in my success. For whatever reason, I have always believed that my big ideas would work, and, most often, they did. Some of my businesses have definitely been more successful than others, but I made them happen no matter what anyone thought. What stops many people is that they don't believe strongly enough that their idea will work, so they never break through a certain point of resistance.

You become what you believe, not what you think. There's a subtle but profound difference between the two. Our thoughts form our beliefs. We have so many thoughts every day, and many of those are negative. The more common a thought, the stronger it becomes, turning into a belief that can subconsciously control our lives. We're not usually taught to pay attention to thoughts unless we purposely seek out instruction on doing so. But cultivating awareness is the first and most important step. Thinking particular thoughts is just a habit, and habits can be changed.

What you repeatedly—consciously or unconsciously—tell yourself becomes your reality. If you surround yourself with people who share similar limiting beliefs, the situation escalates. There's simply no way around this fact because we live in a vibrational-based reality. Knowing it can be overwhelming and scary, especially if you need to make some drastic changes, but you are reading this book because you sense what's possible, and every day you'll get closer to making it happen.

For example, it was when I started paying attention to how I was thinking that I noticed Low and High Jenna, and I realized that if I let Low Jenna have too much control, I wasn't going to get anywhere. When Low Jenna had the wheel, I felt physically tired and dull. That was my signal to switch gears. I would stop what I was doing, take a few deep breaths and repeat an affirmation to myself. If Low Jenna was thinking, "I've got too much work, I'll never get it all done," I'd consciously switch the thought to a thought like, "I'm going to do this in the time I have and do it brilliantly." I might have to repeat this many times throughout the day before the new thought took hold, but eventually it would. And, amazingly, that dull feeling would shift too. Suddenly, there would be room for inspiration and I would feel energized again.

I encourage you to try this. Start paying more attention to how you're thinking and feeling. Try this the next time you notice a pervasive state of "Low You":

1. Note how you feel in your body, mind, and heart.

2. Note the thoughts associated with your feelings. Is there something you're saying to yourself or a way that you're thinking about a situation that's bringing you down?

3. Change the thought by replacing the negative one with something positive as many times as you need to, to change the pattern.

4. Pay attention to any shifts in your experience when you change the way you're thinking.

By acknowledging how powerful your brain really is, you can shift your world in the most profound ways. If you've done any self-discovery work, you're likely very familiar with this concept. And there's a lot of power in revisiting the idea. Repeating steps like those above gives us the power to choose our thoughts and sculpt our beliefs, becoming the strongest, best version of ourselves.

CASE STUDY
Rachael Hatala of Laughing Sparrow
(laughingsparrow.ca)

A relatively new Makie, Rachael has *so* much positive energy and has been killing it at the shows in Vancouver, Calgary, and Edmonton. Whenever I walk by her Laughing Sparrow booth, it's bumpin' with eager customers crowded around it. Although she hasn't been in the community for long, she's already integrated and many Makies are inspired by her because she levels up each year. I'm such a fan of Rachael and love to hear her updates because she shares stories of reaching a new milestone every time I see her. Her story is also relatable.

Rachael has been making things her whole life. Her first crafting memory is of extracting beads from a three-inch-high orange shag carpet and then stringing them on dental floss to make a necklace when she was a toddler. Her family was also very creative and, by buying her art and craft supplies instead of toys, encouraged young Rachael to make things. She was raised by a single mom who taught her to dream big, so when Rachael was 12 years old she decided to start her first business. Her grandmother lived and owned a store on Mayne Island off the coast of Vancouver. Rachael had noticed a growing trend of wrapping beach glass in wire to create pendants and earrings, which she decided she could also make. She spent hours scouring the beach, collecting pieces, and turning them into jewellery that she sold in her grandma's shop, feeling delighted when people bought them. Filled with encouragement, she approached other stores that might want to carry her designs. The shop owners weren't interested in selling product made by a kid, but she did not let that deter her. While on the ferry to and from the island, Rachael imagined her jewellery one day being sold in the boat's gift shop—a dream she still has today.

As a kid, one of Rachael's favourite games was pretending she owned a store. She wrote out orders and believed that one day she would be running a shop in real life. In her early 20s, Rachael returned to her love of crafting and dabbled in cross-stitching, knitting, and other activities that kept her fingers busy. She worked part time at a hobby/craft store and got in trouble for helping customers too much. To help pay the bills, Rachael also bartended on the side. She didn't know what move to make next, but then her boyfriend (who is now her husband) bought her a silversmithing course that would change the trajectory of her life.

When Rachael completed the course, something clicked into place. Even though it challenged her perfectionistic ways, she realized she could apply what she'd learned to a business that she could make money at while she continued to learn new skills to materialize her ever-changing design visions. This inspired her to spend $10,000 on supplies. She didn't have the money, so she had her mom co-sign a loan. Her mom was skeptical but recognized Rachael's passion and decided to go along with it.

With all her tools, supplies, and gear, Rachael was ready to make it happen. She set a goal for herself that she would sell $10,000 worth of jewellery. This goal took five years to reach. She did it by selling to customers at the bar where she still worked part time, along with two other jobs. They would see what she was wearing and want to buy pieces for themselves. When Rachael finally reached her goal, she rewarded herself by buying a pair of $800 Christian Louboutin shoes while in Las Vegas.

Rachael's first show was a quilt show that her grandmother had organized on Mayne Island. The show was small, but it gave her a taste for what was to come. When she took a break to have her daughter, Sofia, her husband, Martin, stepped up to support the family. At first, Rachael thought that she would want to stay at home and home-school, but after eight months she sat down at her jewellery bench one day and cried, feeling as though she had come home. She had to get back to making.

When Sofia was a year old, Rachael sent in applications for several shows, including Make It. She wasn't successful at first, but at the last minute, she was accepted into a local show. She knew that even though she didn't feel ready, it was an opportunity she had to say yes to. This was her big break and the first show at which she made some real money.

Rachael had another big break at Make It—not in her own booth but while she was there helping out a jeweller friend. Even though Rachael hadn't been accepted into the show, she wanted the opportunity to be part of it in some way. That year, we decided to offer guaranteed acceptance to the next show. The Makie who Rachael was working for didn't take us up on the offer, which gave her an idea. Toward the end of the show, she asked if I had time to chat. I did, and she began to tell me her story and how much she desired to be a Makie. As I listened, I couldn't help but see how genuine she was. She even began to tear up because she wanted to be part of Make It so badly. I'm a big softy and immediately started to cry too. I couldn't help but offer her a spot in the upcoming show. When I did, she gave me the *biggest* hug and a thoughtful gift. Well-played, Rachael.

Rachael continues to kill it at Make It Vancouver, Edmonton, and Calgary, and this warms my heart to the core. She always has a huge smile on her face and enthusiastically tells me all the exciting things she's up to. Her line, Laughing Sparrow, came to be sold in 30 stores and her goal for 2017 was to be in over 50. In 2015, Rachael did $42,000 in sales and decided to set her goal for 2016 at an impressive $100,000. Not only did she make it, but she slaughtered it with a whopping $150,000! Because 2016 was such a gangbusters year for Laughing Sparrow, Rachael decided to fulfil another dream and take her family to Europe for a month. Festivals she participated in paid for the trip. Martin was also able to quit his job to stay at home with little Sofia so that Rachael can make more jewellery.

It's such an exciting time in Rachael and her family's life, but she feels like she's drinking out of a firehose sometimes. She often thinks back to the early days when she was figuring out how to make everything work. Today, she has the confidence to do anything. Not only does Rachael make all the jewellery for Laughing Sparrow herself but she also mentors other jewellers. She's passionate about sharing her skills with budding makers who have the same infectious enthusiasm. In the beginning, she said yes to absolutely everything that came her way, but she's reached the point where she's so busy that she has to say no to some opportunities.

What I love about Rachael's story is that she kept going for her dream despite initial rejection. Like so many of us, one of her biggest fears is rejection, but she also knew that she wouldn't get ahead if she let it stop her. There were scary, awful, and hard moments, but she is so clear on her vision that she's always able to refocus on what she really wants. What's also amazing is that making jewellery is one of her greatest joys in life. She was born to do it and has stopped at nothing to make it happen.

Here are Rachael's best tips for making it happen:

- If you never try, you'll never figure it out. The more you build this muscle, the easier it gets.

- Jump before you're ready and don't say no to the things you want because you're scared.

- Don't stop in the middle just because it's hard. You're usually closer to the end than the beginning, so keep going.

- Give yourself regular reality checks. Focus on your progress rather than how much you need to do and assure yourself that you're doing fine.

- There's only so much you can do and it's crucial that you're always your authentic self.

- Don't put other people on a pedestal because their lives look perfect on social media. Chances are they think that your life looks perfect too.

- To make it happen, you just have to do it. Put one foot in front of the other and focus on what's right ahead instead of the entire mountain.

- You can't build a house with a screwdriver, so make sure you learn the skills you need to know to get where you want to go.

- Surround yourself with people who want to see you succeed.

- Treat your competition with kindness. There's enough to go around, so just focus on what you're doing and don't worry about everyone else.

- Celebrate milestones by buying yourself awesome shoes!

It's Not About How Hard You Work

From a young age, most of us are taught that the harder we work, the more success we'll have. This is true, but only to a certain extent. Think about people you know who work tirelessly but never seem to get ahead. You likely know other people who don't seem to work very hard at all, but they constantly travel and do other fun things with their lives. Leading up to Make It, I work very hard, but I've also created a life in which I have a lot of autonomy to travel the world.

I've always had a belief system that allows me to see the world differently. I don't think that the only path to a successful life is to work my ass off for someone else. I'm convinced that I can do what I enjoy *and* make money.

This isn't a belief system that I learned growing up. Both my parents were from hardworking, middle-class families, so their story was that you had to get a job with a big company and work your way up. But this never felt true for me. I tell you this because I want you to know that it doesn't matter what your beliefs were as a kid—or what they are right now. It's possible to change no matter how old you are or how stuck you might feel. We can adapt and overcome pretty much anything.

You get to decide how easy or hard things are going to be. For example, have you ever had to do something that you knew was going to be really difficult, but you felt so pumped about doing it that, in the end, it actually felt effortless? Or maybe there was a tiny, insignificant task that shouldn't have caused much trouble but doing it took loads of effort?

Our experiences are shaped by the emotion and energy that we apply to them. When you're pumped up and excited to do something, it's enjoyable, and no matter how much physical and mental effort it requires, you can do it with ease.

Sink or Swim

Generally, there are two reasons why people don't live the life they desire:

1. They don't know what they want.
2. They're too comfortable to change.

Comfort can be an amazing feeling. I mean, who doesn't want comfy shoes? But it can also cause stagnation and, eventually, depression.

Humans are hard-wired to grow. Maybe you've heard the phrase, "If you're not growing you're dying." It sounds a little over-the-top. But something slowly dies in us if we aren't willing to evolve. You just have to look at nature to remind yourself how normal evolution and expansion is. But evolution is uncomfortable, which is why so many people avoid it. We love familiarity and consistency. They make us feel safe, as though we're in control. A level of certainty *is* necessary for well-being. But if comfort becomes too much of a good thing, we run into trouble. This is generally true of anything in life. I'm pretty sure you could overdose on green juice and yoga if you really wanted to prove a point.

If we outgrow a situation, at first we usually deny the truth. It can be scary to realize that something you're used to no longer fits. This often occurs in relationships. If you're evolving faster than your friends or romantic partner, you get to a point where you have to make a decision—yes or no—are they depriving you or inspiring you to go after what you really want in life?

Things that are right usually feel good. If something doesn't feel good, there's usually a reason for it. I call these "yes feelings" and "no feelings." Sometimes I get tripped up with a "maybe feeling," but experience has taught me that a maybe is usually a "no" in disguise. When you're presented with a situation, an opportunity, a potential collaboration, or something else, and—even if it looks terrific on paper—it just doesn't feel right, your intuition is telling you something's off.

What can be tricky is identifying the difference between a no and fear. This takes practice, but the more you make decisions that are in alignment with your yes and no feelings, the easier it becomes. For example, in the beginning, I said yes to every speaking gig that came my way because I was so keen to get up in front of people. Over time, I've become more discerning about what I agree to, and I've noticed that often when I say no to a speaking gig that doesn't feel aligned, another one shows up that does. But if you go against your intuition and later regret it, try to forgive yourself and be open to what the situation has to teach you.

When you're beginning to make it happen, you will be tempted to say yes to *everything*. It's important to have this attitude because it can give you a lot of momentum and forward velocity. But you'll reach a tipping point at which saying no to certain things will notify the Universe to give you less of that kind of opportunity and more of the kind that fits where you're at and where you want to go. Sometimes you have to draw a clear, firm line in the sand and declare what you are and are not willing to do.

Integrity

Ultimately, you have to keep your promise to yourself to make it happen. No one is responsible for your life but you. The more you're able to grasp that, the freer you'll be. When you stop seeking approval, permission, and acknowledgement from others, a whole new world opens up. There's *so* much freedom in committing to yourself above all else.

Keeping our word to ourselves can be one of the hardest things. We get caught up in habitual behaviour patterns. A harmful habit is about not being in control of an impulse for something desired. Usually the urge is for destructive behaviours like smoking, gambling, gossiping, and doing drugs.

To change a bad behaviour, you have to replace it with a good one. Who thinks this is *way* easier said than done? If this were a breeze, wouldn't everyone just switch their cigarettes for carrot sticks? You can't change your behaviour unless you change your beliefs. Keeping your word to yourself means you follow through on what you commit to.

It's easier to break promises to yourself than to other people because no one is keeping you accountable. When you tell a friend that you're going to do something for them and you don't, they usually get frustrated with you. But we do this to ourselves every day. Think about it. If someone repeatedly lets you down, eventually you disconnect because it starts to feel too crappy. You can't trust them, so you don't feel there's much point in maintaining the friendship.

Yet you may do this to yourself constantly. Each time we don't take action on our dream, we break a promise. We create cracks in our foundation and eventually these take their toll. We lose confidence in our ability to achieve our goals. Many people carry around this wound. When we deny ourselves the opportunity to make it happen, we let ourselves down. Show up for yourself as though no one else will.

The Person Who Will Change Your Life

There's an Instagram meme that says, "If you're searching for that one person who will change your life, look in the mirror." This struck a chord with me and, according to social media, with many others too. Often, we think someone else should tell us how to do it, sign our permission slip, or decide on the value of us or what we create. But no one out there can do this for you.

As you make it happen, there will be many moments when you must decide on your course of action, regardless of what anyone else thinks. You determine your path. You won't be an asshole about it, hopefully, but living a life for someone else's approval will never give you satisfaction. In turn, people will express opinions about whether or not what you've decided is good for you, but their words are, in fact, simply a reflection of what they think is possible for themselves. If someone believes in their own greatness, they will be able to see that in you too. Try to associate with these types of humans.

There's no better feeling in the world than accomplishing the thing that you set out to do. This is why you hear people say, "I did it for me." They kept a promise to themselves and had enough love and commitment to be accountable to themselves. Making it happen comes from a deep, grounded place like this. Sure, you could perform like a monkey and make tons of things happen for other people. We've all done it. But it doesn't offer the deep sense of satisfaction of doing what you've longed to do for yourself, even if there were many uncomfortable and brutal moments along the way. Difficulties don't hold so much sway when you're committed to doing it, no matter what.

A good friend of mine is a prominent psychologist in Vancouver. She's one of the smartest, hardest working, badass boss ladies I know and constantly makes many things happen. Right before she turned 40, she randomly saw an ad for a body-building competition and decided to get in the best shape of her life so that she could enter. She is not someone you'd imagine participating in a bikini fitness competition, but she was attracted to the challenge because it provided her with a goal to work toward.

To prepare, she had to work out for hours a day with a trainer and eat basically only chicken and veggies. She stopped drinking and rarely came out on weekends. Her friends had no idea what she was up to because she didn't tell a soul about it. The goal was for her alone, so she kept it on the down low. It wasn't until she achieved her goal in the competition that she decided to shock everyone by posting on social media some photos of her strutting down the catwalk looking buff in a bikini.

I have such respect for people who make it happen for a reason that is deeply personal and not about seeking the approval, permission, or recognition of anybody else. They don't do it to gain more significance or fame. They do it because it's an expression of their soul and because they answered the call to step up and be of service. There's so much power in this because it's authentic and real.

The biggest reason to make it happen is to keep a promise to yourself and express more of who you authentically are as a human being. When you say you want to do something but then don't take action to complete it, you let yourself down and deny the world your gifts. One way to overcome this habit is to consciously enlist other people in your vision. For Make It, the Makies keep me accountable. Otherwise I wouldn't be able to pull it off. Considering your work a group effort that serves the community can help enormously with accountability.

The Power of Words

Words have power. They become our thoughts and, once congealed, those become beliefs that dictate our actions.

Pay careful attention to the language you use and notice if certain phrases are habitual. Even if you use them jokingly, negative sayings about yourself can stick. Ones to watch for are "I never have enough time / money / energy to . . ." or "I wish I had . . ." or "I can't seem to . . ." Speaking in negative absolutes, using words like always or never is a sure way to solidify beliefs.

Ask your close friends to help you spot negative patterns in your speech. They might be able to identify something you had *no* idea you do regularly. It can be hard to hear the truth, but it really does help end patterns that don't serve you.

Set High Standards

A lot of people set low standards for themselves and many times they don't even realize it. As Tony Robbins teaches, when you are willing to accept anything, you don't attract the best. Usually people who have awesome lives set high standards for themselves. They aren't willing to compromise for anything less than what they truly desire and feel they deserve.

Only you can set your standards. They're deeply personal and will evolve over time. Your standards are a reflection of you and the values you live your life by.

Make It Real

To change beliefs, you have to pay attention to your current actions and default settings. The more conscious you are, the easier it will be to shift and move forward.

1. Pay attention to your thoughts. When you notice a negative thought pattern, choose an affirmation and consciously use it to replace the negative thought. For example, if you hear yourself thinking something like, "I'm not good enough," you might choose an affirmation such as, "I am valuable and I have an important gift that will serve others."

2. Commit to fulfilling a promise to yourself about something you want to achieve. This could be a promise you haven't yet been able to keep. Write it down on a piece of paper that you stick up on the fridge or in your office, somewhere you'll see it every day. If you feel tempted to break your promise, stop what you're doing, read

the promise, and recommit to it. You may want to ask a trusted friend to help you with this. Tell your friend about your promise and ask if you can call on that person to help you keep it by reminding you of all the reasons you made this commitment to yourself.

3. Pay attention to your speech. The next time you're talking to a friend, notice if you habitually say anything negative about yourself. For added awareness ask your close friends to help you spot negative patterns in your speech. They might be able to point out something you had *no* idea you do regularly. Even if it's hard to hear and you might feel self-conscious, the truth will set you free.

4. Make a list of your standards. What do you want and what are you unwilling to accept any longer?

Six

Making It Happen: Getting Into the Flow

. . . .

"There is no scarcity of opportunity to make a living at what you love; there's only scarcity of resolve to make it happen."

WAYNE DYER

THERE ARE PRACTICAL things that you can do to get into the flow of making it happen and staying there for the ride. When you are in this state for a length of time, a total transformation occurs and your way of being in the world drastically changes.

Even so, you'll probably never feel like you've fully arrived. Each thing you make happen is only a moment in time. When we reflect on life, we often see that things we thought would fill us with happiness didn't. While sitting at a boring nine-to-five job, you might have imagined that once you quit and started your own business, you'd feel like you'd finally arrived. When you left the job and felt the same way, you might have told yourself that once you earned a certain amount of money, *then* you'd finally be on top of the world. Making it happen is not about striving—it's about what you feel in this moment. The journey is a non-linear cycle. I consider it a spiral staircase. You go around and around, hopefully in an upward direction. The staircase looks like this:

STEP 1. You have the initial inspiration for what you want to make happen.

STEP 2. You feel excited and tell people about your vision.

STEP 3. You create a plan.

STEP 4. You take the preliminary actions to get started.

STEP 5. You start.

STEP 6. You progress forward.

STEP 7. You get blocked or challenged by something.

STEP 8. You figure out what to do next and move forward by learning a new skill or way of thinking.

STEP 9. You get a boost from something magical, spontaneous, amazing.

STEP 10. You repeat Steps 6 to 9 as many times as needed.

STEP 11. You get to the top and are ready to do the entire process over again.

You might get caught up at each step. Some levels will be easier than others, depending on what you're trying to accomplish. You've likely made some things happen with total ease and few challenges. You were in the flow.

Step Up onto the Spiral Staircase

When we're working toward a desired goal and seeing results, we usually feel fulfilled. Life has magnetism. Happiness can be defined as the perception of progression toward a worthy goal. We decide the worthiness of our own goals. Overall, people would feel much happier if they made more of their heartfelt desires a reality. Life is short and it goes by quicker every day. Sharing your inspiration will light up everyone who resonates with what you create. The world needs this positivity now more than ever. Contributing what brings you joy is a vital thing for you to do with your life.

If you're holding this book now, it means that you're curious about your full potential. You're also reading it because I decided to make it happen. I had to overcome deep insecurities and self-doubt to manifest it, but I did it to inspire you. One of the most profound ways we learn is from each other. If no one was willing to share their talents, we would likely still be living in caves and gnawing on raw meat for lunch. Sharing our talent is scary, but it's also rewarding. Plus, we only have one life, so we may as well see how big and bold we can live it.

How do you take that first step, especially if you want to accomplish a lot and you're not sure how to start? Observing how others make it happen is inspiring. They seem to be lit up from inside and able to do anything they set their sights on.

A coach once told me to start only projects that I was in love with and enjoyed doing with all my heart. I had several things on my plate at that time and I had hired her to help motivate me to complete them. When she suggested I reflect on how much I wanted to do these things, I questioned her ability to coach me. I didn't realize that she was actually testing my motivation and determination to persevere when the going got tough. For each item on my to-do list, she asked me to rank from 1 to 10 my commitment to completing it, and if I didn't immediately shout out, "Ten!" she'd ask me if continuing with it was the right decision.

Review your own list of priorities in this light, and then take a step up onto the spiral staircase.

Make a Plan

If you don't have a plan, it's almost impossible to take action. As a highly creative person, you might find it difficult switching from the right side of your brain (the artistic/intuitive side) to the left (the analytical/rational side). Planning is a left-brain activity, so it can seem tedious to creative types, but it is the crucial infrastructure for the dream you're building.

Devising a plan to realize your vision requires reverse engineering, creating a strategy from your end-goal to your first move. Here's one approach for how to start:

1. Do a good ol' brain dump. Take *all* the shiny, pretty ideas in your head and put them on paper.

2. Make it bold and colourful. Use felt pens in a massive sketchbook or on another large surface. You might draw diagrams or use photographs or other visuals to represent parts of your plan. Get messy and have some fun.

3. Use moveable parts. Record aspects of your plan on sticky notes so that you can move them around like puzzle pieces as it starts to take shape. This can serve as a reminder too, to be flexible and open to new ideas and opportunities as they come up.

If you're working on a project you've never done before, sometimes the next step is not obvious, so it's important to seek out people who can help you. There's always a way to figure something out, but you may have to be particularly resourceful. Good thing we can always ask our friend Mr. Google. Even if what you're making happen is unique, chances are the process of doing it is not. Others out there have experience that you can benefit from. I highly recommend that you don't do it alone.

Even When Things Are Wrong, They're Right

Things can go wrong (or at least not the way you expect them to) and making it happen usually takes way longer than you planned. This is totally okay, but people often worry or make situations hard when they don't have to be. Approach life in a lighthearted, playful way so that you can rise above difficult situations much more easily. You have full control over how you respond to everything that happens. In traffic jams, some people get completely pissed off, honking and swearing, while others turn up their music and groove in their seats. Everyone's in the same situation but their experiences are completely different. Be the person who dances hardest, whatever the situation.

Ask *any* entrepreneur and I almost guarantee that they'll say the early days were the hardest, and the most fun and rewarding. All sorts of unpredictable opportunities and outcomes are available, as is the magic of blind uncertainty. It's a lot like the euphoric feeling of falling in love. You don't know much about that other human, but you rush toward each other with reckless abandon. You let your guard down and expose who you truly are. There's the same delicious openness at the beginning of making it happen. But this can lead to uncertainty and shakiness at times. Let's consider a few reasons why.

The Wobble

Making it happen requires you to open your heart and be vulnerable. It's scary and uncomfortable to feel so exposed. This is why the majority of people work in jobs that they don't like so that they can make enough money to enjoy leisure time. Even if what you're trying to make happen isn't going to be your full-time gig, you're expanding into a realm that requires you to wobble. This can be uncomfortable, but like trying to balance on a ball at the gym, the more you wobble, the more you build the muscles to stabilize.

No wobble
= no
growth.

You might feel a little wobbly just thinking about your big, beautiful idea. Often at the beginning of a project, I feel a tiny bit nauseated. 99% of me is pumped when I visualize my goal, but 1% is scared out of my mind. It's truly excitifying (exciting + terrifying)! If our goals don't make us queasy, we're not dreaming big enough.

Only You Can Give Yourself Permission

Remember asking for your parents to sign permission slips for school field trips? Unless you had a signature (forged or real) you weren't permitted to go. You've got to sign your own permission slip for life. If you wait around for someone else to sign for you, what you want likely won't happen. That's why I asked you to sign at the beginning of this book. With your commitment, you've signed your own permission slip.

Start Before You're Ready

It's rare to feel 100% ready for something new. You'll never have all the answers and you probably don't know half of what you need to. But you can figure things out along the way. Not having all the answers keeps you on your toes and allows you to learn important lessons as you go. If you already knew everything, where would you find motivation to do anything at all? What would be the point? The fun is in everything you discover on the journey.

If, right out of the gate, I had planned to create a massive craft fair, I would have been too intimidated to start. Because I focused on each individual step, the show was able to grow in stages. The trick is to allow your business—and life—to unfold naturally and not push anything. Think of it this way: if you planted seeds in the spring, you wouldn't dig them up every day to see if they'd sprouted. You'd water them and make sure they got sunlight. You'd give them love, and they'd grow when they grew. Making something happen is like this. You show up, work hard, do the things that you say you're going to, and then have faith that your dream will grow. If you force things along or grip too tightly to ideas about what you think should be happening, your project will stagnate and you'll eventually kill the idea.

Inspiration versus Motivation

Inspiration is a magnificent thing that gives us the juice to create. When you're a creative entrepreneur reliant on generating fresh new ideas and concepts, you need to take inspiration seriously. Otherwise you dry up and your work becomes stale and uninspiring to you and your customers.

Ever wonder why your best ideas seem to pop out of nowhere, like in the shower when you least expect it? You're lathering up your hair and—*bam!* —you have a brilliant idea just like that. Inspiration strikes when you're in the moment, tapping into a divine connection. So don't overthink it. Inspiration shouldn't be tamped down with our small-minded, limiting beliefs.

In our day-to-day lives, with smartphones, social media, and news breaking online, things move pretty damn quickly. You can do almost everything you need to do from a computer or even a cell phone. Advancing technology is a tremendous thing, but even more so is taking the time to slow down and listen to your inner wisdom. It has insights for you that aren't available anywhere else. If you can't hear them, it's likely because everything around you is so loud.

We distract and over-stimulate ourselves with these gadgets and endless, irrelevant information. As a result, tapping into that knowing part of you becomes more difficult. More often than not, we're working from a left-brained place of motivation rather than the intuitive space of inspiration.

Working from Motivation

A common belief of Western society is that we must work hard to get something, that the key to success is to be motivated, set goals, and push ourselves to get there. If you apply this practice, you will undoubtedly be successful, but you might not enjoy it all that much if you're working from a place of motivation rather than of inspiration. It can be easy to confuse the two because on the outside acting from one or the other looks the same, but inside the experience feels very different. The end-goal could also be similar, but acting from inspiration will allow you freedom, and acting from motivation will shackle you with constraint.

Working from motivation focuses externally and has a lower-vibe feeling:

- We set our targets by other people's standards.
- We follow all the rules.
- We stick rigidly to the decided-upon plan.
- We overly focus on the desired result.
- We care a little too much about what others think of us.
- We consider the work hard but something that must be done.

Motivation is applied by an outside source, such as a parent, teacher, or coach. It can also come from peers and friends. Athletes are taught to be motivated to win. In school, we're told to do our homework and score well on exams. Think back to when you were a teenager. For many of us, what we wore, our activities, and who we went on dates with was motivated by what other people thought of us.

Working from Inspiration

Inspiration has a higher vibe than motivation because it comes from within and from the heart and has nothing to do with what other people think. It feels like a pull rather than a push. It's bright, clear, beautiful, and full of light. Inspiration opens you up to possibilities that exist beyond anything you could conjure on your own.

Working from inspiration is a response to an inner calling and has a higher-vibe feeling:

- We listen to our unique inner spark to help guide our decisions.
- We set our own rules.
- We have a plan but stay open to intervention from the Universe.
- We know our vision is as much about the process as it is the final result.
- We care first and foremost about what the person in the mirror thinks of us.
- We feel jazzed about the work that we're doing.
- We love our lifestyle.

When I feel inspired about Make It or anything else, I'm on fire and everything feels possible. It's like there's a big, delicious vegetarian meal in front of me and all I want to do is fill my body up with its nourishment. Inspiration is one of the highest vibrations we can experience. It makes you feel like you're flying.

You can't force inspiration or talk yourself into it. Falling in love or asleep is similar. There was a time in my life that I suffered from insomnia and every night I tried to make myself fall asleep, which made the insomnia much worse. Inspiration is about allowing a feeling to permeate you. It's listening to the subtle sound of a voice that hints you toward where you should go and what you should say and to whom. It's an undeniable impulse that guides you to unforeseeable, serendipitous moments. Motivation will take you part way, then you have to surrender to the energy of inspiration.

Inspiration is boundless, fluid, and physically tangible. It flows from one form to another and gets inside you in a way that motivation simply cannot. It permeates your heart and allows it to sing. It reminds you that everything and anything is possible, and you are exactly where you need to be. In my body, it feels like a spontaneous opening and my heart feels lighter. It lifts me up to a new dimension and allows me to see things I might not otherwise be able to. When it taps on your heart you have to let it inside or it will leave and knock on another door.

Inspiration is our fuel for creating and manifesting ideas, so if you haven't been inspired for a while, it's critical to stop right where you are and immediately do something that brings you joy. This will attract inspiration. It's like a lightning bolt from the Universe, looking for a rod to connect it to Earth and it will pick the path of least resistance just like any form of energy would. Let *you* be the path for inspiration.

Let It All Flow

When you want to make something happen, life can get really exciting. You think about your big idea constantly and likely tell friends and family about it too. They get pumped and often ask for updates on the status of your project. This part is fun, exhilarating, and feels magical, like falling in love. Life seems full of possibilities and promise. You're riding on a high wave; you're energized, filled with almost childlike wonder. The key is to ride that wave as long and as hard as you can. This high-vibing feeling has a lot of power and if you're able to stay there, it can propel you far. Leverage it as much as you possibly can.

When this momentum starts to die down, fear sneaks its ugly head in and starts to whisper little ideas in your ear. These are tainted with negativity and can lead to self-doubt and insecurity. At first it might be subtle, but as time progresses the voice might become louder and more persuasive. Fear has a remarkable power to enter in our subconscious mind and start meddling with our conscious thoughts. One of the results of fear is procrastination. This is such a common human behaviour that I haven't met anyone who hasn't struggled with it. That's why it's so important to know how to keep your inspiration alive.

Fuel Inspiration

Inspiration needs to be fed constantly. Although you can't force it, it's possible to ignite and sustain it. When I'm not inspired, I feel stagnated, dull, and tired, as though I can accomplish only the bare minimum required. It's not very enjoyable. Inspiration, on the other hand, is electric—my batteries are fully charged and I am capable of doing anything. I feel alive and full of the boundless vitality we were put here to experience.

When we're vibing with inspiration, possibilities seem endless. Like most things, this vibe is not constant, but we can be proactive in keeping the inspiration floodgates open. What follows are some of the things that feed my inspiration. I share them with you so that you can reflect on what fuels you.

Listen to Others

One of the best ways to inspire myself is to simply listen to people who I admire and who have accomplished things that I really want to do. We're very lucky that there are so many ways to access excellent podcasts and videos featuring some of the world's greatest minds. I love to fill up my brain with their stories of triumph but also of their struggles to get where they are and how worthwhile the journey was for them, because it reminds me that if they can do it, I can too. Plus, it opens my mind to a vast array of possibilities I might not have considered, especially when people speak vulnerably, from the heart.

Be in Nature

Connecting to the greatness of the natural world fills me up in a profound way. Anytime I feel in a funk, I go outside and allow myself to explore and open up to the wonderment and beauty. Being outside, breathing deeply, and opening my eyes widely rejuvenates me. No matter how blah I may feel, being outside and moving my body always improves my mood.

Explore

I love to travel. Arriving in a place that I've never been before opens my mind and ignites an indescribable feeling deep within my soul. A fresh perspective on the world is electrifying. Observing people live their lives is what I enjoy most. The little things like how they drink their coffee or what they eat for lunch. I love learning new customs and traditions so that I can try them out and see how they feel. When I'm at home in Vancouver, I explore different parts of town and new restaurants. Doing something outside your normal routine forces your brain to think differently and experience something new. Our experiences shape us, and when you get too rigid about how you're experiencing life, inspiration doesn't come so readily. It's as though inspiration lives outside us, and to let it in you have to create the space.

You don't need to hop on a plane to get this rush. Just do things you don't regularly do. Try a new restaurant in an area of town you rarely visit or go to the art gallery and see a new exhibit. A day trip to a place you've always wanted to see but have never been could also help you get fresh perspective. For added results, wear a new outfit and do your hair differently.

Create with Inspiration

Without inspiration, you won't get the fresh new ideas to make a product people will connect with. When you don't feel inspired by what you're creating no one else will either. A different energy suffuses art and products created with inspiration. When I walk around Make It, for example, I can feel the pull of certain booths. The Makies with passion for their product communicate it on many levels, from how they set up their booths to how they package their goods to how they sell them. Stepping into their booths feels good because the positive energy they radiate is attractive. You may have experienced this when you've entered a place and immediately felt happy. You might have bought a bunch of things that you weren't initially planning to. You couldn't help yourself but you didn't totally know why.

That's experiencing the radiant inspiration of the maker. You can't help but be attracted to it because it makes you feel something enjoyable. Their energy connects with yours and the positive vibration is palpable. They've hit their stride and are in their flow. They let passion flow through them and the result is customers give them money hand over fist. Nothing fills my heart with more joy than seeing a Makie fly.

I've been fortunate many times in my life to achieve this positive pull. I recall being at craft fairs with my Booty Beltz and being beyond thrilled. I loved my product and couldn't wait for other people to enjoy it too. I would give every person who walked by a very enthusiastic demo. I felt this unstoppable force of excitement that I wanted to share with the world. At most shows I didn't even have a chair. I would stand for up to 11 hours straight. My enthusiasm annoyed a few of my neighbours, especially when they saw all the Booty Beltz I sold. Some were shocked by how well I was doing. There can be such a high in sharing our inspiration with others. It's a magical loop of positive feeling that benefits everyone involved and that's how the currency of abundance flows.

CASE STUDY
Diana Luong of Craftedvan
(craftedvan.com)
. . . .

Diana's is a story of creating with inspiration. Growing up in Vancouver, Diana was artsy and loved to make things like painted rocks that she gave to her parents as gifts. She also liked playing video games with her friends in her free time.

Diana recalls her parents being supportive of her artistic talents. When she was in grade 4, she designed graphics and gave them away through online contests on the primitive social media platform Asian Avenue. She didn't make money from this venture but she learned a lot by doing it. It gave her confidence in her ability to design.

In high school, Diana designed posters for performances for the theater department. She loved creatively expressing herself through her designs. A friend even mentioned to her how passionate she seemed to be about design and that she should think about studying it. In theatre, Diana met her future business partner, Erica, and they became close friends because of a shared love of crafting. They spent hours together making things for themselves and friends.

For her post-secondary education, Diana chose graphic design at Simon Fraser University. She and Erica had regular crafting nights and continued to explore their creativity through making. They took a leap of faith and signed up for a craft fair at the university, curious to see if anyone wanted to buy their wares.

So that they could create more inventory, they went to the dollar store and spent $50 on all sorts of craft supplies. Erica had a passion for knitting and Diana created some magnetic bookmarks. Together they created as much stock as possible and had a very positive experience at the fair. With a big smile on her face, Diana recalls selling their first $10 knitted hat and being over the moon with excitement, even though it took Erica five hours to create it.

They began selling at other shows and it became apparent that the bookmarks far outsold knitted products, so they decided to focus on the bookmarks. In 2013, they named their business Craftedvan and created an Etsy store. A year later, they finally had the confidence to post things on it.

On completing her degree in graphic design, Diana began interning at Hootsuite, which led to a full-time job in community development. As much as she enjoyed working at this rapidly growing tech company, a series of serendipitous events led her on a new path. I feel fortunate to have been one of the people who helped steer Diana toward following her bliss.

A colleague of Diana's at Hootsuite was also into the handmade community. She approached me to create an evening for crafters called Hootup Craft. I agreed to meet with her and Diana for lunch. I immediately liked Diana and was thrilled when they asked me to help them organize this event, which turned out to be a success.

Exhibiting at Make It was a dream for Erica and Diana. In 2014, they applied and were accepted. It was a big deal for them and they sold far more than they ever thought possible. Since Craftedvan was rapidly growing,

Diana reduced her hours at Hootsuite to part time. It was only a matter of time before she would consider quitting altogether.

I had recently bought Chandler out of Make It and posted a job on Facebook that Diana claims couldn't have been more perfect for her. I still remember the day she messaged me and said she was the person for the job. During the interview, I hired her on the spot.

It was challenging for her to make the leap and quit her secure job at one of Vancouver's largest tech companies and work as a contractor in a tiny office in Gastown, but she hasn't regretted the decision for a moment and has been a big part of Team Make It ever since, helping to take our branding to the next level. I'm so grateful that Diana messaged me that fateful day because I don't know what I would do without her. Working for Make It has also afforded her a lot more time for growing Craftedvan, whose bookmarks, greeting cards, and magnets are now sold at more than 50 stores around the world.

Diana and Erica developed a thriving Etsy business and have an impressive social media following. Their customers love them and are a big reason why they continue to be successful. Diana and Erica have a ton of supportive friends who help them make and sell their bookmarks at shows. Their business would not be what it is today without this help.

In 2017 they took a big gamble and signed up for the National Stationery Show in New York. Although it wasn't as financially successful as Diana would have liked, it was a rich learning experience that they could only get by trying it.

Up until the summer of 2017, their headquarters

had been in the living room of Diana's parents' home. Although Diana's parents didn't object, she and Erica found their own office space so that they didn't have to worry about overtaking the entire house as their business grew. Working in a more professional environment has upped their game.

Craftedvan has also grown by trying new things. In 2016, they created a subscription service called Read Happy Plan. Customers sign up online to receive a selection of bookmarks each month. Their fans are book nerds and love being surprised with new designs in the mail. Avid readers are a community in themselves and by tapping into this group, Craftedvan has built a tribe of super-supportive and enthusiastic customers.

As the business continues to grow, Diana and Erica have had to figure out the delicate balance between working on their passion and at part-time jobs to pay the bills. It's not always easy and many days it feels like there aren't enough hours to get everything done. Luckily for me, Diana has never regretted quitting Hootsuite to work for Make It because she's able to be so flexible in pursuing her passion. There will come a time when Craftedvan calls to Diana full time, and it will be a bittersweet day for me.

Here are Diana's best tips for making it happen:

- Pay attention to what people tell you you're best at, as these words might be clues to your passion and future direction.

- In the beginning, let your creativity flow. You can always edit later.

- If you're not having fun, don't do it. This doesn't mean every day will be easy, but if what you're doing doesn't light you up, it will be impossible to get through the challenging times.

- Follow the signs, even if they don't initially make sense.

- Engage your friends and family in the process. They will want to help you if you tell them how best to support.

- It's okay to be scared when you're first starting out.

- Find your niche and love it up. The book nerds love Craftedvan because Craftedvan loves them back.

- Don't be afraid to take a leap of faith. It might not pay off the way you expect, but if you don't try, you'll never know.

- If things are getting too serious, lighten up and figure out a way to have more fun.

Keep It Real

When you're making it happen, it's important to stay grounded. A daily practice can help keep you in the flow. I encourage you to incorporate one, all, or a variety of the practices that follow into each day. Before long, you'll experience the results and be hooked.

Meditation

Meditation is one of the best ways to stay grounded. For example, I practise something called Transcendental Meditation, which uses a mantra. I do a 20-minute meditation every morning when I wake up. When I remember, I do one in the afternoon too. This allows me to tap into my guiding system and clarify my intentions and what's important. When I'm quiet and still, I can hear more clearly. There are many different kinds of meditation, so explore until you find what works best for you. Apps and YouTube videos can help. The most important thing is that you do it.

Breathing

Being aware of your breath is one of the best ways to get through challenging times. For me, breathing is one of the best techniques for changing how I feel and managing stress. In 2016, I worked with a breath coach and the experience radically changed my life. It can be easy to ignore something that we naturally do, but if you want to increase your energy, I recommend looking into pranayama breathing, kundalini yoga, or shamanic breath work. There are lots of YouTube videos to help you. Or seek out different classes to discover the best method for you.

Dancing and Moving

The older I get, the more important it becomes to incorporate daily stretching and movement into my life. If I skip a day, especially if I'm working on my computer, I notice it big time. You don't have to be a gym person, just dance or move around for at least 30 minutes a day and you'll notice a significant difference in your physical, mental, and emotional well-being. It doesn't matter if you aren't a great dancer. Put your favourite music on and groove. Yoga is another great movement practice. There are so many different types and the benefits are overwhelmingly positive. Some of the best business ideas I've had occurred to me while I was sitting on my yoga mat, and I know I'm not alone in this.

Eating More Plants

The more plants you eat, the better you'll feel. You don't have to give up pepperoni pizza, but I highly encourage you to pay careful attention to what you eat while you're making it happen. What you put in your mouth and how often has a profound way of shifting how you feel. Good stuff in, good stuff out. When you're working a lot, it's awfully tempting to eat food that tastes delicious at the time despite it not being healthy for your body. You don't have to be completely hard core about it, but if your diet needs improvement, now's the time to do it. Your body and brain will perform at a much higher level if you nosh on food grown from the earth.

Writing

Writing things out on paper helps you release what you don't want to hold on to and to see life from a different perspective. You can take a step back from your thoughts and evaluate them. It's also fascinating to reflect on the formation that happens with life experience. When you write it out, you can trace the dots that have connected in sometimes unexpected ways. Incorporate journaling into your daily practice to understand yourself better and also to be able to see how far you've come. Who knows, maybe you'll want to share your findings in a blog or in a book someday!

Creating a Make It Happen Schedule

In 2012, I had the great privilege of working with a wonderful coach, Marie Forleo, during her Adventure Mastermind program. She would often say, "If it isn't scheduled, it isn't real." This is so true. When you bring your creative idea to life, if you don't have a clear picture of what to do next, it's easy not to do the work at all. Writing down a schedule that includes all your tasks is a means of holding yourself accountable.

It's okay if your schedule changes but make one to keep yourself on track. Knowing what you're going to do and when means you'll worry less and be more likely to stick with a plan. Scheduling will help you slay your to-do list with ease and grace.

Learning

Reading, watching, and listening to things that are in alignment with what you want to achieve speeds up the process of making it happen. It's crucial to constantly prime the pump by consuming the right types of information. To be a more effective learner, try to absorb only information that will take you to a more aligned way of being. Stop reading low-vibe articles and watching TV that uses negativity for entertainment. You don't want to live in a bubble, but be mindful of how much you consume because it can be harmful to tap into the collective consciousness if it's overly negative. Also avoid having surface-level conversations. Not much is more dulling than small talk with people you're not interested in connecting with. Have deep, soulful conversations that inspire you to be a better version of yourself.

Paying Attention

Pay attention to your life, particularly to what you consume. Think of yourself as a Ferrari. What kind of gas are you going to put into your tank and how will you take care of your engine? If you treat a Ferrari like a Toyota, it's not going to perform at its optimal standard. From food and information to what advice you follow and what stimulation you expose yourself to, the more mindful you are in your choices the more you'll feel the benefits.

Taking Care of Yourself

We've talked about this before, but it is very important, and therefore worth repeating. Taking care of yourself can be hard when you're busy. Eating crappy food, not exercising, and forgetting to meditate feels excusable when you have a lot on the go. But slacking on self-care is a big mistake. If you become tired, run down, and feel sick, it's much harder to get things done. Cutting corners on your self-care routines might seem like saving time, but before long it catches up with you. It's like the old airplane mask analogy: you can't serve others if you don't serve yourself first. Plus, it's impossible to feel good about your business if you don't feel good about yourself. What you are radiates from within and is felt by everyone around you.

With this said, don't put too much pressure on yourself. Some days you'll slip and that's okay. I'm an overachiever, so I'm innately hard on myself. But I cut myself more slack these days, which in itself is a practice of self-care.

Self-care means different things to different people. You need to define what works best for you. I encourage you to get to know and commit to your own self-care routines. Remember to choose things that benefit your mind, body, and spirit. If you are feeling strong and alive, your life force will be unstoppable!

Spreading Good Vibes

When you spread good vibes, you attract good people to your life and good customers for your business. You are probably loyal to brands, stores, and restaurants because of how they make you feel. Good and bad energy can emanate from inanimate objects like websites, menus, and hang tags. Everything we create reflects a message that can be perceived by your customers.

There's a slogan that says, "Your vibe attracts your tribe." This simple statement has a lot of truth to it. Your business is a reflection of your vibe and that of the people you employ. If something isn't built on a positive foundation, it will never last. If you are a high-vibing person, it's not likely you'll attract a low-vibing customer, and if you do, they won't stick around for long. The opposite is also true.

The more layers of your inauthentic self you shed, the more high-vibing you become. Inauthenticity is based on a feeling at the core of who you are. No one can decide if you're being authentic or not—only you can tell. And it's possible not to realize you're being inauthentic. Don't beat yourself up if it's taken a long time to get to know your authentic self. You're awake now and that's all that matters.

People don't intentionally decrease their vibe, generally speaking, but it can happen without awareness. Subtle slips of your thoughts and day-to-day behaviours can add up and if you're not careful, you can unconsciously change your frequency. The only way to combat this is to have regular check-ins with yourself. A simple question to ask in any given situation is, *Am I feeling expanded or contracted?*

Your answer will give you the feedback you need to change your behaviours, thoughts, and beliefs to get back up where you belong.

Infuse Your Work with Love

When you feel love for what you're doing, it supercharges possibility. Love is a strong force whose vibration lets you accomplish so much more. It's not *always* possible to love what you're doing, but you can train your brain to love *more often* with some simple techniques.

Keep a Gratitude Journal

Every day, write down 5 to 10 things that happened that you feel grateful about. Consciously taking the time to slow down and notice is very powerful, and your gratitude will open life up in profound ways.

Use a paper journal, your phone, or another device to keep a separate gratitude journal specifically for your business. At the end of each day, write down a few things that you're grateful for that happened in your business. If your day is rough, this might be difficult, but do it anyway. If stuck, consider what your life would be like if you were in a nine-to-five job that you hated instead of being your own boss. Maybe you had a job in the past that you didn't enjoy. How much better is your life now compared with then?

Cultivate an Attitude of Gratitude

Beyond the journal, cultivate an attitude of gratitude. When things go right, bask in that glorious feeling. Exaggerate it as much as you can to feel the positive vibes intensely. Play with it. Stretch the gratitude out for as long as you can while maintaining an authentic feeling of it in your body.

When someone does something that makes you happy, thank them and tell them how much you appreciate their kindness. Maybe your new intern goes above and beyond what you told them to do or a new store places an unexpectedly big order. Whatever the case, do something extra-nice for them in return so that they feel your appreciation. The more you feel love, the bigger it grows, and things have a way of working out more smoothly and joyously. When you have a consistent attitude of gratitude, things start to go your way more often than not, and bad, stressful days become a thing of the past.

Choose How You Feel

You choose how you feel about your business. Some days I wish that someone would step in and take charge. Being a boss has its challenges and it would be so nice not to have that heaviness on my shoulders. But then I remember that it's my ship and a big part of why I'm steering it is because I get to run the show and make the decisions. It's powerful to take full responsibility for your attitude. Don't make the mistake of getting caught up in the low vibration of feeling sorry for yourself because you're stressed out, tired, and have too much on your plate. You've created your business, so take full ownership for it.

Not taking responsibility for your life is a trap that many people get caught in and it keeps them small, stressed, and unhappy. The "poor me" game doesn't serve anyone—especially not them. When you throw a pity party for yourself and invite all your friends, you'll probably get the response you're looking for. Many people will sympathize with you, particularly if they aren't living the life they want to live. Secretly, when you complain about how hard being an entrepreneur is, they will feel justified in their own decision to not take the plunge. This is why finding a tribe of like-minded business renegades is vitally important. They will help you get through the tough times and give you a kick in the ass when you go down to negative town for too long.

Starting a business that supports your lifestyle is a beautiful privilege. In fact, if you have the means to start a business, you're luckier than most on this planet. Many would love to be your in shoes, so be a glowing representative. The world needs more inspiration, beauty, and love. Light and positive energy radiates from people who do the work they're meant to do in the world and choose to feel good about it.

Fill Up

The things you think, do, and believe are like tiny drops in a bucket. Having a negative thought here and there isn't a bad thing, but if they become regular occurrences, the wrong bucket will fill up.

Research shows that the average human has between 50,000 and 60,000 thoughts a day. The frightening truth is that 95% of those are the same that we had yesterday. Yikes! Unless you make a conscious effort to change how you think, your monkey brain will repeat the same thoughts . . . again and again and again.

Breakthroughs, epiphanies, and aha moments occur at rare times when the brain thinks something different than it thought in the past. These moments excite us because they help us soar over hurdles that have tripped us up before. It can feel like we're passing a new level in a video game. They often happen when we feel relaxed and open. Let your brain download information that will allow you to experience life in a whole new way.

Make It Real

Clarity is key to determining the right opportunities to seize and directions to take. When you regularly attend to your vision, it becomes stronger and your belief that it's possible becomes more real.

1. Make a plan by following steps 1 to 3 on page 112. Make space in your plan for new inspiration and information to enter in. When you believe it, you'll see it, so get as clear as possible about what you want to manifest.

2. Sign up for a learning opportunity. Be it a business course, a meditation class, a guitar lesson, or something else, choose an activity that inspires you.

3. Keep a gratitude journal for your business. At the end of each day, write down 5 to 10 things that you're grateful for that happened during the day. After writing down each point, close your eyes, take a deep breath, and revel in how good it feels.

4. Each month, read one book that resonates with you because you know it will take you closer to your dreams. Commit to doing all the exercises (just like you're doing now)! Better yet, invite a friend or two to read the same books and form a book club to discuss them.

Seven
What to Do When It's Just Not Happening

. . . .

"If you really want something, you can
figure out how to make it happen."

CHER

O N YOUR MAKE it happen journey, you will hit road blocks. Even when we do the work and try to stay out of our own way, inevitably something comes up that seems to prevent us from going to the next level. I know this frustrating feeling all too well. But with some awareness and understanding we can bust through all that sticky resistance.

Face Fear

. . . .

Fear. A four-letter word. We can use another four-letter word to tell this one where to go. No matter what, fear will squeeze its way into your life, especially when you're about to have your biggest breakthrough. You can't really do anything to stop it, but you can do a lot to make sure that it doesn't crash the party when you're making it happen. No one invited it, so don't let it through the front door. And get some big, burly bouncers to smack fear around a bit when it tries to sneak in through the back.

Sometimes fear is totally warranted, like when a crazed, rabid animal is running toward you, showing a mouthful of teeth! In this case, fear saves your ass by giving you superpowers to outrun the beast. For this, you'll thank fear because it possibly saved your life. Fear acts like your BFF when you meet someone and automatically feel a little frightened of their scary vibe. Your instincts are telling you to say no, thank you, to anything this person wants to sell you. You'll tip your hat to Mr. Fear, once again, this time for helping you live a happy life without a creep pulling a fast one on you.

Lots of books, videos, podcasts, and so on claim they will help you fight your fear and get rid of it once and for all. It might sound awesome to walk around without fear, doing all the scary stuff you want without feeling like you might barf. Sign me up! Unfortunately, if you eradicated your fear, you likely wouldn't be a fully functioning human and would end up somewhere unpleasant, like behind bars. So we don't want to get rid of fear, we want to prevent it from controlling us.

Fear is like an overprotective parent. My mom was a bit like this when Chandler and I were growing up. I was the oldest child, so I broke the rules sometimes to prove that she was overdoing it. (Chandler, you're welcome!) I had to learn to push back so that I could express myself in my own way. You can deal with fear similarly. When it acts like an overprotective parent, tell it to chill out and then do what it's trying to stop you from doing. Almost always, it's not nearly as scary as your fear made it out to be.

Fear wears lots of different sneaky disguises, and you might not always be able to identify when it's being over-protective. Awareness is the best way to discern what fear is up to and call it out in its tracks. Fear means well, but as someone who desires to make it happen, you have to push past it to get what you want and live the life of your dreams. You have to identify where fear hangs out and what costume it's wearing at any given moment. Here are some of the out-fits that fear keeps in its closet.

But I'm a Perfectionist

Oh, snap. This is a tricky one! Many of us are held back from making it happen because we want it to be perfect before we share any of our work. If only we had a little bit more time, money, talent, energy, and so on, then it would be per-fect and we could finally follow through on our idea. Sound familiar? Chances are it does because this is a *very* common fear in disguise.

Perfectionism is kind of sexy. People think that you're extra-special because you only share things that are at a super-high quality. It's common in job interviews to slide in that your biggest weakness is your perfectionism. In other words, you have extremely high standards that even you can't reach. It's concerning that this is seen as a positive thing.

I'm not a perfectionist and never have been. I'm a little sloppy at most things I do, and that's why I've been able to make a lot of things happen. I used to envy perfection-ism and wish that I had inherited that angelic trait too, but now I'm glad that I didn't. In the beginning, each of my businesses were pretty shaky. My first Booty Beltz were held together with glue! But they still sold, and eventually I had a lot of success. The first Make It shows were very far from perfect too. I didn't know what the heck I was doing a lot of the time, but I did the best I could and, miraculously, it worked out. Maybe this is the reason I'm a spiritual person. I had to believe in something higher than myself or I would've been hooped.

Recognizing perfectionism for what it is will help you move past it. If you're reading this, chances are your standards, abilities, and resourcefulness are above average. When you get down on yourself and think what you're doing isn't good enough, just remember that you're already ahead of the curve, so your average is better than most people's great. I'm not encouraging you to be arrogant, just be grateful for your gifts. Denying them is just fear wearing a different outfit, trying to get you to waste more of your precious time and energy. You don't want that, so don't go there!

If you doubt what you're doing is good enough, ask people who truly want you to succeed for a smack down. They will give it to you because they love you. Let them show you what they see and be grateful for it.

It's Too Hard, It Will Take Too long, It's Too Complicated...

It's too hard, it will take too long, it's too complicated, and the like are super-convincing excuses and people love to sympathize with you about them, especially if they're trying to avoid doing something too. Usually the things you really want to do in life aren't cakewalks. If they were, you'd have done them already and a bazillion others would've too. The bell curve exists for a reason, and that you get to determine where you'll be on it is excitifying. Most people are comfortable right in the middle, and that's where they stay. Totally fair, but I have a feeling that you wouldn't be happy there.

Doing worthwhile things always has its challenges. But if the outcome strongly compels you, you'll move through the barriers to it. Plus, moving through the sticky resistance is how you get all the learning and growth.

If I Fail, Terrible Things Will Happen

I've failed many times, and the worst that happened was that I lost some time and money. That's a small price to pay for what I learned. People fail at things every day and hardly anyone bats an eye. They are usually focused on their own lives that most of the time they don't care all that much about what others are doing. When you see someone fail, do you think they're a loser? Probably not. You likely think they're brave for trying in the first place. This is what people will think about you if you try to make it happen and don't succeed the way you'd have liked. If anyone thinks otherwise, it's probably because they don't have the guts to go after their own dreams. Mermaids don't pay attention to the opinions of shrimp.

Others don't see your failure the same way you do. You see everything you did wrong and all that you could've done differently. How someone else views your failure has a lot more to do with them than it does with you. There are people out there that will never take a big risk in their lives because they're too afraid of what other people will think if they do it wrong. They will be the first to criticize when someone else gets it wrong because that proves their theory that it's best to not start in the first place. The Internet labels these people trolls. Do you really care what someone like that thinks about you? If you do, *stop*.

Smart, kind, talented, successful people don't spend their time bringing other people down. Instead, they lift others up. The people who matter and who you ultimately want to impress will look at anything you create as a valiant step forward. They want to see you succeed and likely know from their own experience that it doesn't happen overnight. Failure is a way for us to learn and to reflect on whether we want to move forward despite the setback.

One thing to watch is that you, yourself, don't act like a troll. When you see people kill it, consider them an inspiration because they've proven it's possible to get to that level. Check in about how you respond to other people's successes and failures. Do you think and act in alignment with how you want others to see you? If not, correct your course.

Failure is such a gift. It doesn't always feel good when it happens, but with time, it's usually possible to see the beauty in it. If we never failed, life would be so predictable. There wouldn't be any sparkly magic. Failure is an opportunity to go in another direction that usually leads somewhere you wouldn't have chosen on your own. Making mistakes shows you what you need to know and the areas where you need to grow. When you fail, you can throw your arms up and say a big thank you to the Universe for having your back and helping you be the best you can be.

Fear and Self-Worth

One of our biggest fears is that we aren't good enough, so we're constantly looking for ways to validate our worth. This is why social media has caught on like wildfire. It's an instant-gratification mechanism that validates whether we're doing an okay job at life and are liked by others. The problem starts when you rely on it to determine your self-worth. There are many more meaningful ways to feel a sense of value than the number of likes on your photo. It might feel warm and fuzzy at the time, but the buzz doesn't last long. How *you* feel about *yourself* is paramount.

There's nothing wrong with looking outside for validation, but it's good to know why you seek it. Oprah once said that after every interview—whether of movie stars, rock stars, or royalty—without fail, the interviewee asks her if they did okay. Even Beyoncé! We're not alone in our need to measure up, but that we feel deep levels of inadequacy is sad. Why don't we give ourselves more credit for being the magnificent creatures we are? At least when we shine the big awareness light on this issue, we can see it for what it truly is and loosen its grip.

We tend to be intimidated by our own power, glory, and greatness. We want to be good enough and at the same time we're scared of being too great. How weird is that paradox? We are *so* smart yet do all kinds of silly things to sabotage ourselves.

CASE STUDY
Chandler Herbut of Ole Originals
(oleoriginals.com)

Chandler, my brother, is one of the savviest entrepreneurs I know. He's a shining example of someone who put fear aside and was willing to take a big risk when he was starting out.

Chandler is a natural leader and salesperson. When he was in elementary school, he was part of a fundraiser for his hockey team, raising money by selling chocolates. Chandler outperformed all the other kids on the team and won a hockey jersey as a prize. One of his first jobs was as a sales clerk at Sport Chek and, once again, he was the top seller, making a solid paycheque for someone his age because of his commission bonus.

Our dad is the founding partner of a prominent commercial real estate company in Edmonton and it was always assumed that Chandler would follow in his footsteps. But after training for this, he had a change of heart and decided to move to Vancouver to work for a marketing company. He enjoyed the job, but after a while it didn't fulfill his need for creativity. He began exploring different hobbies.

Chandler worked the door at the first craft fair I started, Stop & Shop. About a month before our holiday show, he told me he was going to start a T-shirt line so that I could cater to the many bored-looking dudes at the show who had nothing to buy. I thought he was a bit crazy because there wasn't much time to produce them, but I agreed to give him a booth.

This was 2007 and Ed Hardy was all the rage. Chandler wasn't a fan of the garish designs and wanted to create T-shirts that were simple and slim-fit. Like me, he has a love of travel and so he wanted to incorporate heritage and culture into the design. Because people usually have an emotional connection to the place they're from, he wanted designs that would resonate and connect people to their roots. He worked with a graphic designer to complete the designs and then invested in inventory for his first time selling at Stop & Shop.

Unfortunately, when the show began, no one stopped or shopped at his booth, and he was devastated. My heart broke because of the time, effort, and money he'd invested in his new business. But then something shifted and people began buying. By the time the show ended, he'd made a nice profit and was hooked. His next stop was the One of a Kind Show in Vancouver. He was also busy creating a website and online store for his company—Ole Originals—named after our grandfather Ole, which is also Chandler's middle name.

In 2008, Chandler became more involved with helping me create Make It. Ole was quickly growing too, and he was less interested in his job at the marketing company, so he lowered his hours to part time and then decided to quit.

This was a turning point for Chandler and me because we had to grow the business so that it could support both of us. The early days of Make It were fun, exciting, and scary. We didn't really know what the heck we were doing as we embarked on an eight-year journey that established Make It into what it is today.

In the early days of Ole, Chandler focused on menswear but soon the ladies wanted to buy his simple, clean designs for themselves. He began making screened hoodies and tank tops. He'd been outsourcing the screen printing to a local company, but he wasn't happy with the final product, so he decided to invest in his own equipment. The second bedroom in my Gastown loft became the Ole Originals factory/Make It office. It

wasn't always easy for Chandler to balance both businesses because they were growing so quickly.

Eventually, to get more separation and increase production, Chandler rented a small studio space devoted
to Ole. He hired his friend Mandy to help him sell at
shows and do screening. In 2013, a much larger studio
space became available. To make it work, Chandler sub-
let part of the space to other local artists. Make It also
made the new space its headquarters until Chandler and
I parted ways in 2016. During those times it was often
challenging for Chandler to divide his focus, but he was
committed to making it happen, so he figured out how
to structure his time efficiently and effectively.

Inspired by the 2010 Olympics in Vancouver and
all the patriotic pride, Chandler made Ole a true Cana-
dian brand. The most popular shirts are in a line called
Places. These non-touristy shirts with the slogan "Love
where you're from" tap into hometown pride for the
cities and provinces that have helped to shape Canadi-
ans. For Canada's 150-year anniversary in 2017, Chandler
designed shirts that represented our country in a way
that was stylish and tasteful. He knew they would sell
well, but sales exceeded his expectations by 400%! Ole
had a record online sales day when the Canada 150 shirts
were released.

Stores constantly sell out of Ole shirts. Even though
the T-shirt market is very competitive, Ole has steadily
grown since 2008. Chandler attributes his success to
a few factors. Since the beginning, quality has been a
priority. Chandler also consistently engages with customers by featuring them on social media, interacting

with them at craft fairs, and inviting them to his studio sales. Because everything is printed in-house, he can be flexible and adaptable with his designs. Ole now has four part-time contractors and Chandler is building his team to facilitate more growth.

Writing Chandler's story has filled me with so much big-sister pride! We've both been on a wild ride of entrepreneurialism since we were little kids in Edmonton. Those early business attempts planted the seeds for what we'd later do in life. Almost every day, I spot someone in Vancouver wearing an Ole Original, and that my brother is the creator of the shirt puts a smile on my face.

Here are Chandler's best tips for making it happen:

- When you get the creative impulse to do something, just do it!

- Don't worry about not having all the answers when you start. They will come as you continue to pursue your goals.

- Get to know as many other entrepreneurs as possible so that you can learn from one another.

- When you care about your customers and engage them on a regular basis, they will help you figure out how to serve them best.

- Have faith it will all work out.

- Get yourself as organized as possible in the beginning and as you go create systems for later growth.

- Hire slowly, fire quickly.

- Create a business that allows you to live the life you want to live. Bigger isn't always better.

- Set goals because it feels really good when you destroy them!

Procrastination

Procrastination will get in the way of making it every time. You know there's something you should and maybe even want to do, but it's as if there's an invisible force pulling you away from the task at hand.

If you want to make something happen, why prevent yourself from doing it? While writing this book, there were several days when I set up my writing space, made my tea, lit my scented candles, opened my laptop, and couldn't get anything done. It felt even worse when I reminded myself that I was writing a book intended to help people make it happen!

There are some things that no other person on the planet can help you do. One is living your life. Another is creating your art and growing your business. Sure, once the ball is rolling, you can hire a bunch of people to help execute an idea. But you, the visionary, have to birth the creation into existence. No one else sees it the way you do.

We procrastinate because we're scared of what we'll create. We worry that it will suck, that it will be too amazing, or that it won't get any recognition at all. The outcome of putting your heart and soul into the world is unknown, no matter what stage of the game you're at. When you're starting out, you don't have a benchmark, so the first thing you release sets the standard that you'll go up or down from. Undoubtedly, your product will be judged and you have no control over the reception of it.

Procrastination is normal, and if you have creative ideas that you want to manifest, you'll have times when you procrastinate. When you do, take note and ask yourself why you're putting off the work. The answers will be there for you. Listen for the gentle answer from within. For me, procrastination is a response to the fear of being seen. I crave attention, but if it gets to be too much, I freak out and want to hide away. This stems from being shy as a child. I've outgrown it, but there's definitely still a bit of shyness at the core of who I am.

Dance with Procrastination

A fun way to deal with procrastination is to give it animal, monster, or gremlin characteristic. My procrastination is a foxlike, charismatic game-show host, a total smooth talker like Fantastic Mr. Fox. I want to do something, and I say I'm going to do it, but Mr. Fox sweetly manipulates me into doing something else. He's so charmingly deceitful that often I don't even see him at work until after the fact.

For example, I plan to write, set up everything to do so, and, all of a sudden, Mr. Fox appears with a shiny idea about an activity that's way more fun. He even makes it seem legit, convincing me that it could contribute to the project I'm working on. "Jenna, darling," he says, "this is research." Next thing you know, I've been on Instagram for 45 minutes. Not helpful!

Outside Pressure versus No Pressure

When there's outside accountability, pressure surges through us and pushes us to make it happen. But when you work for yourself and don't have to report to anyone, you often don't have that outside pressure. This is especially true when you're first starting out. No one knows what you're capable of (including you!), so you don't necessarily feel the squeeze to perform at a certain level.

I need accountability, so I always build it into my projects. For this book, I hired a team to keep me on track to meet my goal. If I hadn't had a hard deadline, there's a high probability that you wouldn't be reading this book now. It's the same thing for Make It. There's a schedule that needs to be followed so that the show will be successful.

When we want to make something happen, we often doubt it will make a difference in the world. We can be *so* passionate about an idea, but it's common to assume that it doesn't matter much whether we carry through with it or not. That's why it's helpful to know why we do it:

- We do it for others.
- We do it for ourselves.
- We do it to prove that we can.

Our creative visions have meaning and make a difference in the world. When we do things to inspire others, a positive ripple effect occurs, magical things happen, and the world is elevated.

Understanding why you want to make something happen will help you get through the sticky times when you feel like you can't go on. Ask yourself, *What's more important than doing what I love and knowing in my heart that I'm meant to be doing it?* Are Facebook, Instagram, or video games more important? *No.* There's nothing more important than your vision. You'll be a better parent, partner, and friend when you're on a path that speaks most clearly to you.

Make Time

As with anything, you have a choice about how you relate to time. It can either be your friend or your *frenemy*, work for you or against you.

The cool thing is that you can make time just like anything else. To bring your goals to fruition, you have to intentionally carve out time to do the work. Despite how clear your vision and plans are, if you don't dedicate time in your schedule to executing them, they won't happen. Sometimes you have to turn thoughts like "I should do this" into "I must do this" for the gap in your schedule to appear. Otherwise, something else will always take priority.

When I'm making something happen, if I'm smart about how I spend my time, I usually discover I have more of it than I thought. Like any currency, time is something that we get to spend in different ways. The best part about it is that we all have the very same amount and can choose how we allocate it.

These days there are *so many* delightful time-wasters that seem innocent and even productive. Social media is a big one. Think of all the things you could've made happen by now if you'd dedicated the same amount of time to your goals as you have to looking at silly cat videos. To make it happen, you have to put yourself on a clean diet of productivity and cut out the crap that takes you off your game. I'm not saying that you shouldn't indulge, every once in a while, in watching videos of adorable kittens and puppies making friends. But be mindful that how you fill your time when you're not working can serve to raise you up rather than weigh you down.

When I'm on social media to engage with the Make It community, seeing all the great Makie photos and witnessing their excitement for the upcoming show is inspiring and useful; but otherwise, I don't spend a lot of time there because I look to other things to fill me up. My philosophy is to use social media without having it use me. My method is called "post n' run." I post photos because it's a convenient way to archive memories and share what I'm up to, but I resist being sucked in.

Clean Out Your Life

A 60-second Oprah video has been floating around the internet. In it, she basically says that to get to a high level, you must cut certain people out. She talks about doing her own cleaning out of people and how it changed her life.

You have to be responsible for your own energy—and for others when they're not responsible for themselves. Negative people literally suck the life force out of you. Only distance from them will protect you. I'm sure you can think of at least a few energy vampires bringing you down. It's *not* easy to clean them out, and it's hardest when you're in a romantic or familial relationship with someone like this. They likely have no idea they're doing it either.

After you see friends, ask if they've inspired you or tired you. Of course, sometimes people have stuff like breakups, sickness, or family situations come up in their lives. If they're down for a while, it's understandable. But some people suck the life force out of you no matter what.

The most important consideration when cleaning negative people out of your life is to do it from a place of love and kindness. Be gentle with people's hearts. They are delicate and tender, and I would never want to hurt someone from a lack of consideration or empathy. If you must have an uncomfortable conversation with someone about your decision to cut them out of your life, give that person so much love and compassion. Honour them for who they are and where they are because there's no need to be mean or hurtful. How you treat other people says a lot more about you than it does about them.

When you're in high mode, the only people who can help you up to the next level are others at your level or above. The ones below can't do it, so stop looking to them for help. Keep in mind, this has nothing to do with how someone looks, how much stuff they own, or their status in life. It's all about their attitude and the energy they put into the world. To discern whether someone is a good mentor/friend or a harmful one, look for signs and trust your gut. You have to find the balance between giving someone a chance and trusting how you feel. Our gut instinct is so wise. The more we listen to it, the further we get in life.

Be the Elephant

Low vibrational people create noise and distraction because they're yelling at you from below to get your attention. I love the saying, "The elephant walks on as the dogs bark from below." Be the elephant and keep walking no matter how yappy and annoying those dogs get! Stooping to their level won't help any of you.

The elephant/dog analogy applies to other people but also to the relationship you have with yourself. While making it happen, you'll switch from dog to elephant multiple times. The high version of you will slowly and steadily march forward while the low version bites at your ankles.

Haters Be Hatin'

Haters hate because it's easier for them to tear you down than it is to bring themselves up. Usually, these people haven't accomplished anything significant and instead of facing their fears and working hard to accomplish something big, they seek satisfaction by using negativity to bring others down.

People are more aware of haters now than ever before. Social media has a lot to do with this. The way people put each other down with a click of a button disgusts me, especially when I see women tearing one another apart. It's gross, completely unnecessary, and a massive waste of energy and time. Ladies, let's work together to lift us all up.

When you become more successful, haters will emerge. You don't have control over that, but you do have complete control over your reaction to it. This knowledge offers a lot of power and comfort. When we encounter a hater, we can decide how and if it will impact our life. Instead of buying into someone's online negativity, we can take the perspective that the reason they're attacking us has nothing to do with us. They're in a place of pain, and they're trying to bring us down so that we can share in their negative experience. Hurt people hurt and free people free.

We don't attract haters because we're doing something wrong but because we're doing something right. We have taken the excitifying leap of faith and done something awesome that's beyond ordinary. If you're reading this book, it's because you are extraordinary. You have a unique, valuable gift. Not only were you able to discover this gift but you have the courage, the dignity, and the humanity to share it with us all.

Develop deep empathy and compassion for haters so that you don't waste time and energy blaming them. See them where they are and consider how it might feel to be in that position. If and when you see your first negative review or comment, consider who wrote it and where they might be in their lives. When you can offer them compassion, it takes the sting out of a spiteful comment. You don't have to take it in because it's not about you and not yours to take. Leave it where you found it. That's exactly where it belongs.

Self-Imposed Limitations

If you believe you're only able to achieve a certain level of success, you'll prove yourself right every time. It's only when you challenge yourself to go beyond a certain level that you can see new possibilities. Check in with yourself from time to time to make sure you aren't limiting yourself.

In school, we're taught that being an artist isn't a "real job." It might be a fun hobby or an enjoyable pastime, but we're encouraged to go for jobs with steady paycheques and benefits. It's no wonder that so many artists, makers, and crafters have a complex around money and pricing their work. We're taught from the start that it's not a viable way to earn an income and this gets ingrained in our belief system.

Unless we become role models and inspire others to see that the starving artist mentality is bullshit, it will continue. Through my own experience and from observing others who participate at Make It, I know that it's possible to live an abundant life by selling what you make. But we must decide what we want and commit to settling for nothing less.

Before 1954, everyone thought it was impossible for a human to run a mile in less than four minutes. Many tried to beat it, but an invisible ceiling prevented them from breaking it. Then, on May 6, 1954, Roger Bannister ran a mile in 3:59.4 and everything changed. After that, many people ran a mile in less than four minutes and today the record is 17 seconds faster!

I see a lot of artists brush up against a similar dynamic. Based on what they see around them, they falsely believe that only a certain amount of success is possible. Their conversations are about the struggle, which serves to strengthen it. The thoughts we have most become our beliefs, and these become our reality, so when all we think about is how hard it is to make money, we earn accordingly.

Decide how much money you're going to attract. If you're happy with a little bit, there's nothing wrong with that. There are many kinds of abundance, and the phrase "lots of money" means something different for everyone. Like Notorious B.I.G. said, "Mo Money Mo Problems." But I encourage you to examine your beliefs around money because they might not even be yours. Much of what we think about money comes from our parents and others around us. If your parents always believed that making money was difficult, you may think the same way. Maybe they said, "Money doesn't grow on trees" or "Rich people are assholes." It's possible to have picked up on these beliefs without realizing it.

If all your friends are starving artists and you suddenly start to kill it and make a lot of cash, some weird jealousy will almost certainly start to percolate. Your friends might not even know they feel this way. They'll say they're supportive of your success, but there's a chance you'll feel an odd, passive-aggressive energy that you can't quite put a finger on.

If you sell at craft fairs and are obviously doing well, some exhibitors may feel threatened by you and make comments that don't feel so good. When I was selling Booty Beltz, I did extremely well at craft fairs. My product wasn't particularly amazing and my booth usually looked rough around the edges, but I was passionate about what I was selling and customers could feel it. I recall a few people saying things that weren't nice and hearing about gossip spread about me. It's so important to remember this fact:

What people say and feel about you has more to do with them than it has to do with you.

If someone in your life doesn't have a lot of self-awareness, they might feel threatened when they see you "living the dream," and take it out on you. This kind of behaviour is completely unjustified. You don't deserve it and it's not right. But humans are complicated creatures and their behaviour can be quite confusing at times. I have had a few challenging situations in which people have acted downright mean because they were jealous of my success. These situations were hurtful, but I've learned from successful friends and peers that they too have experienced similar situations.

A moment comes when you realize you can make it happen. You see the finish line and you know you're close to the end. You did what you set out to do. When this happens, you'll have manifested your ideas into reality by:

- Co-creating with the Universe to share your gifts with others.

- Developing awareness of your thoughts, knowing that they shape your beliefs, which become your reality.

- Persevering with your plans while staying open to divine intervention.

- Thinking positively and taking the leap to go beyond perceived self-limitations.

- Believing with all your heart in what you're doing.

When You're Going Against the Flow, Shift

At many points during my entrepreneurial journey, I've experienced struggle. Things just weren't going the way I wanted them to. There wasn't an ease or flow, and I felt like I was pushing every step of the way. I hated this feeling, but for a long time I didn't believe there was any other way, so I just went along with the negative sensation. Many people around me seemed to be having a rough go too, which made it feel justifiable.

Where you're at in your business is because of what you believe to be true. This is why some people with awesome product don't do as well as others selling things that are mediocre. Their success is about what they believe to be true for themselves. Ease stems from believing something will naturally unfold the way it's supposed to, without a lot of brute force or wasted energy. Often, even when we understand this concept, we feel frustrated because we don't know how to change our thoughts so that they translate into the beliefs we desire.

A variety of techniques can help us shift our thinking. They're straightforward but require a lot of practise. Let's look at some antidotes to that state of going against the flow.

ANTIDOTE 1: Awareness

I can't stress the importance of this one enough. Knowing your "why" gives you the ultimate leverage. Even if you don't fully understand why you're doing something, simply noticing that you're doing it can be useful. Try these steps the next time you find yourself in a negative pattern:

1. Identify the behaviour that's holding you back.

2. Ask yourself why you're doing it. What's the thought or underlying belief behind the action?

3. Decide on an answer that makes sense to you.

4. Take action to change the thought and then change the action.

5. Give yourself so much love and gratitude because this isn't easy to do.

Let's say you notice that any time someone comes into your booth at a show, you immediately grab your phone. If you ask yourself why you do that, you might answer that it's because you're scared to talk to them. You discover the thought behind the action is, "I'm not good at selling." By understanding what might previously have been subconscious, you can now choose an affirmation to counter the thought. In this case, perhaps, "I love meeting new people and sharing my passion about my product." The next time you feel yourself reaching for the phone, you stop yourself and repeat that new thought before making eye contact and smiling at the nice people who've come to visit you and check out your amazing wares.

Here's another example. What if every time you have an appointment with the buyer of a store where you sell, you arrive late. You think about why that is and decide it's because, subconsciously, you feel intimidated. The thought is, "She doesn't like me or my stuff." This is totally fine, and now you've lifted the veil and can deal with the issue instead of hiding from it. You craft your affirmation (for example, "I'm lovable, and I love my stuff") and you set your watch 10 minutes fast the next time you pay her a visit.

You've probably heard the phrase "knowledge is power." Or as Maya Angelou put it, "When you know better you do better." The only way to grow is to have the realization that something is off. This realization comes from reflective work that leads to knowledge and understanding.

ANTIDOTE 2: Self-Acceptance

Letting go of what other people think of you is a tough lesson, but when you focus on what you think of yourself, living your dreams gets easier.

A weird thing happens when we challenge the views that others have of us. The dynamic with certain friends shifts. Some reactions might not be overly positive. This can feel really crappy, especially when you haven't done anything wrong. But it's better to either work through this with friends or let the relationship go, even temporarily, rather than to stagnate. Life gets easier when our energies aren't going into unnecessary struggles.

The cool thing is, the more successful you get, the more awesome people will be naturally attracted to you. I know a remarkable number of kind, successful entrepreneurs. When you sparkle and shine the other unicorns know how to find you!

ANTIDOTE 3: Like-Minded Learning

In my relentless pursuit of learning at conferences, retreats, and events, I have cultivated a badass group of friends. It's invigorating to connect with someone who gets you and when conversation and ideas flow naturally. You could come from different parts of the world, but you share an innate understanding of what makes you tick. I absolutely love this feeling and am so grateful when I meet a new awesome person who's cut from the same cloth.

It's easier than ever to connect with people doing similar things. Twenty years ago, you simply could not meet like-minded people the way you can today. Surrounding ourselves with other positive, supportive, amazing people online or in person keeps a flow of good vibes going—one we can return to if we have an off day.

ANTIDOTE 4: Knowing You're Special, But You're Just Like Everybody Else

On a deep level, we all want to be special, and we *are*, in so many ways. There are some people who you can tell think they're special. Maybe they have a swagger in their step or a confident wink. They've discovered their gift and they love sharing it. This is fantastic and inspiring to see, and we also have to remember that everyone has a special gift, whether they're sharing it or not. It doesn't make them any better or any worse than you.

Keeping yourself in check is very important as you're making it happen. It doesn't serve you to see yourself as either better or worse than anyone else. That's like over-eating or undereating. Neither is good for your health. The balance is between the two.

Blind Spots

That we could be making mistakes without even knowing it is an unnerving prospect. Deep down, most of us want to do everything right. But the fact that *we don't know what we don't know* makes perfection impossible. Because you don't know what you don't know, in order to grow you have to cultivate a level of tolerance for uncertainty and imperfection. It might not be comfortable, but unpredictability makes life exciting.

Uncertainty is wild, volatile, and uncontrolled. Feeling it is what it means to be alive. But if there's too much uncertainty, life can turn into a hot mess very quickly! You can think of certainty and uncertainty like Bert and Ernie from *Sesame Street*. Bert is the quiet, conservative one who always wants a good night's sleep, while Ernie is the crazy wild child. They both play their parts, but to make it happen you have to be a little less Bert and a little more Ernie. Thinking of these conditions as fun characters gives the big, deep-seated emotions they evoke a little less grip.

Along my own journey, I've been stuck many times and not known exactly what to do about it. I could see the block, but I didn't know what was causing it or keeping it there. Maybe you've felt this way too. When you don't know what's holding you back, you can't move it out of the way. To gain awareness and free yourself, you have to get some answers. Ask yourself the kind of compelling questions you would of another person. The more we ask why we feel a certain way, the more answers we receive.

When It's Not Happening

Fully understanding yourself is key to moving beyond your limitations. Whenever your business isn't going the way you want it to or had hoped it would, I encourage you to reflect on these seven key questions.

1. What Is My Desired Outcome?

If you don't know what you want, you'll never be able to get it. I'm sure you've had dinner plans with a friend who's completely indecisive about what restaurant to go to. You ask her what kind of food she wants and she responds with a frustrating, "I don't care." Unless you step up and make the decision, you'll probably wind up at a 24-hour McDonald's because all the other restaurants are closed.

Be as decisive, clear, and specific as possible. Things will likely change along the way, but you have to get the framework solid. Don't limit yourself. Be bold in your declarations. If your desired outcome is way beyond where you are right now, then you have to step up accordingly to make it happen. If you've been a couch potato your whole life and your goal is to run a marathon, you've got to make some *big* changes. A desired outcome has to be something that you can see and believe with all of your heart. Even when you wobble, keep your vision steady. When you can feel it in your bones, you'll know you're ready for the next step.

2. Why Do I Want to Make It Happen?

It can be surprising to discover why we want something. Do you want it because you feel like it's the next logical step or because there's an expectation from the people in your life and your community? Did you make a promise to someone a long time ago that you would do it? Maybe you're trying to prove someone wrong for saying you couldn't do it or challenge the expectations others have of you. The reason doesn't matter—but knowing it does.

When you have a crystal-clear understanding of your motivation, magic happens! It's as if an invisible force were pulling you toward the finish line and opening doors and windows all around you. Without a compelling why, this just won't happen. Simon Sinek wrote an entire book called *Start With Why*, which is testimony to the importance of this question. When you pull the layers back, asking why you want what you want, you discover things about yourself that you might not have known before.

Today, when I ask myself why I made the decision to organize my very first craft fair back in 2007, the answer is because I wanted a market that valued exhibitors and that my friends would want to attend. In many ways, I organized it for selfish reasons. When you long for something that currently doesn't exist, it's a deep desire to change reality. Make It continues to be an event at which creative people make a living doing what they love. I wanted this too, and it's why I continue to do the fair. There can be more than one reason why you make it happen, and it's important to home in on the highest reasons.

3. How Badly Do I Want It?

This one I got from Tony Robbins. After I attended his *Unleash the Power Within* seminar, I signed up for coaching and found an awesome coach who helped me in a bunch of ways. When I told her about the things I wanted to achieve, she consistently asked me about my desired outcome and how badly I want it. By my answer, she could always tell the level of my enthusiasm, and I could too . . . even though I didn't always enjoy admitting it.

At the foundation, you have to want to make it happen with conviction. You have to feel the juice and the exhilaration in your body from the start so that you can tap into this whenever it feels sticky and resistance is kicking in. The more you can feel the electricity of your conviction from the beginning, the easier it will be to tap back into it in the future. When you're starting, savour the full feeling of your conviction and extend it for as long as you can so that it's embedded in your nervous system.

4. What Holds Me Back?

To get yourself unstuck and make it to the finish line, you have to be very honest with yourself about what's holding you back. If you're able to have a full understanding and take responsibility for what holds you back, you'll be able to set yourself free. Looking in the mirror is not easy. But if you're up for the challenge, I suggest you literally go to a mirror, look yourself in the eyes, and ask out loud what's *really* holding you back. Repeat this question until the answers come to you. Don't be alarmed if tears start to flow.

If you answer with a whole lot of external circumstances, call yourself on it! The only person holding you back is you. Yes, there could be a dicey situation and people who are making your life challenging, but you ultimately have control of the situation. That's why Tony Robbins calls his seminar *Unleash the Power Within*. All we need for making it happen is inside us right in the moment.

What ultimately holds us back are beliefs about our own worthiness of love. When I realized this, I felt sad because I could finally see how hard I've been on myself for so much of my life. It breaks my heart when I consider all the pressure I constantly put on myself without giving enough love and appreciation back. If I acted toward another person the way I do to myself, there's no way they would want me in their life.

Your relationship with yourself has to be committed and solid before you try to accomplish big things. A lot of people succeed at many things in their lives but never feel fulfilled because they don't love themselves, so they're reliant on external accomplishments to feel a certain way. They look to the outside to confirm how they feel in the inside. You don't have to make anything happen to be worthy of love. Just being on this planet gives you that right. It's not about making it happen to get more.

5. How Can I See This Differently?

Perception is everything. Thousands of us can experience the same thing, but every one of us will perceive it differently. Just think about movies. Reviewers of the same film often have opposite opinions about it. Not everyone enjoyed blockbusters like *Jurassic Park*, *Back to the Future*, and *Indiana Jones*.

Whenever you feel stuck, scared, overwhelmed, or any other emotion related to fear, ask yourself if you can see the situation differently. Keep asking this question until you get an answer. Eventually something will come up that will take your perception to a higher place. When it does, be grateful for having a better way to look at the situation.

You know the feeling of being head over heels in love, like when you're seriously swooning? If you have this experience, you never forget how wonderful it feels. You look at your lover like they're the most exquisite creation of all time and think that they could never do anything wrong. When you're in this elevated state, you have no worries or cares in the world. It's possible to get yourself into a similar state no matter what your relationship status is.

Remember, the most important person for you to be in love with is yourself. When you're having an extra self-lovey day, consider your vision, what you want to make happen.

Sit with it for as long as you can and with as much clarity as possible. Make notes in your journal or in a voice memo on your phone so that you can revisit them later. The next time you're in a low-vibe place, read or listen to your recording to help shift your perception. When you can remind yourself of what's possible because you've already experienced it, you can bust through limiting beliefs like a boss!

6. What Steps Can I Take Right Now?

When you're feeling stuck, the only way you can get unstuck is to take action. Things only happen when you take steps toward your goal. A runner can't meditate themselves across a finish line. Sure, meditation and visualization will help them get to the end of the race with more ease and grace, but until they put on their shoes and start running they'll never get there.

If you're in a deep state of paralysis and procrastination, even a small, silly task that you could probably do in five minutes can seem impossible. I feel like this all the time and sometimes I laugh at myself for being such a weirdo... even though I know it's totally normal. Why would a simple task that takes only a few minutes be so challenging? Being a human can be so frustrating sometimes!

The momentum of making it happen is like the snowball effect. The more it rolls, the bigger and faster it gets. If you do a few tasks, a natural force will propel you forward. People in business say you either grow or you die. Not many businesses stay exactly the same year after year. The profits either go up or down.

Sometimes you have to get disgusted with yourself to make a change. You go to rock bottom and that shakes you up, so you're forced to do things differently. Drastic weight loss stories always have this component. A 600-pound man who can't get out of bed can't take it anymore and, in a split second, decides to make drastic changes. Doctors may have been telling him for years that he's at risk for premature death, but he has to reach rock bottom to be motivated to change.

You don't necessarily have to hit rock bottom to make a change. But you do have to push yourself to take action when you're avoiding the work. When I have a lot to do but I'm feeling too lazy to do it, I start something totally unrelated to get my momentum going. I'll empty the dishwasher or make my bed so that I have a feeling of completion, which usually kick-starts the momentum for other productive activities for the rest of the day.

7. What Did I Learn and What Am I Grateful For?

If you're not grateful, you can't feel fulfilled. It's that simple. Gratitude is receiving what you've been given. This can be from others, yourself, or the Universe. Gratitude means you appreciate the things that have been provided for you, whether they're what you asked for or not. It's easier to be grateful for what you've always wanted than for what you weren't asking for, but you must be grateful for the good *and* the bad. The things that we don't want shape us into the wonderful humans we become. When I was a kid, I only wanted toys and craft kits for Christmas, and when I got clothes, I was completely ungrateful and pouted in the corner. Now I'm grateful for any gift given to me because I understand it's the thought that counts most.

Gratitude works the same way as love. To feel grateful for other people and situations, you have to first be grateful for yourself. Throughout the day, practise reminding yourself about how lucky you really are. Eat good, clean, healthy food; exercise your body; surround yourself with positive people; allow yourself to enjoy life. And be grateful for who and where you are *now*.

Make It Real

It's time to discover your true why. This is such an important exercise because it gives you amazing clarity for moving forward. Use your trusty journal to record your responses, and for each of the following exercises answer from the heart.

1. Ask yourself why you're doing what you're doing. When you respond to this question, don't try to come up with something that sounds "smart." Just experience the emotions that arise around your answers. Feel what you feel without judgement. The more truthful you can be, the more you can use this feeling as a guidepost for decision making.

2. Examine your beliefs around money. Where did they come from? Do they serve you? Would a shift in your thinking serve you better?

3. When you're having an extra self-love day, ask yourself about your vision and what you want to make happen. Record your answers in your journal or in a voice memo on your phone. The next time you're in a low-vibe place, read or listen to your recording to help to shift your perception.

Part Three

. . . .

NOW IT'S HAPPENING

eight

Grace:
Staying in the Flow

· ·

"It seems like the good things that have happened
in my career are things that you don't try to plan
and push, and make it happen, it just seems to happen."

WANDA JACKSON

N OW THAT SOME of the tough stuff is out of the way, let's look at basking in the beautiful flow of making it happen. Learning how to surrender is huge for many creative entrepreneurs because we're such human *doings* that it's hard to switch off and be a human *being*. Letting go of control can be very uncomfortable, but the more we can surrender, the more intimate with grace we become.

When you surrender, something greater than you takes over and grace flows in. This is exactly what's required at times when you're out of flow and things feel icky. The key is understanding when to put the pressure on and when to ease off. It's like driving a car. If you push the gas way too hard, you'll accelerate too fast and likely do damage.

A lot of people would likely classify me as a hustler. I enjoy the feeling of getting shit done and seeing quick, efficient results. My Make It team and I like to go fast, and it works out well for us. In the beginning, sometimes I would press too hard on that accelerator and I suffered numerous bouts of burnout. Nowadays, I've learned to soften and let go a lot more. If I didn't, I would still be a crazy control freak and no one would want to work for me.

Loosening your grip and surrendering to grace takes practice. If you're an A-type go-getter, it's not going to happen overnight. Taking your foot off the gas when you reach a dead end is a skill you can cultivate with time and awareness. If you've done all you can and you aren't seeing things manifest, it's the Universe urging you to relax into an omnipresent force that's much more powerful than your own.

This book is called *Make It Happen* not *Force It to Happen*. If things really aren't flowing and are making you miserable, it could be time to pivot and change course. Determining this is almost as challenging as distinguishing between danger and resistance when it comes to fear. That's why I can't recommend enough that you cultivate inner knowing.

Only you can determine when and how to do this. Sometimes a simple tweak can make a massive difference.

Set Boundaries

Until recently, I didn't spend a lot of time thinking about my boundaries unless they were crossed. But occasionally things occur that make me re-evaluate whether my boundaries are what they should be. When you're in the process of making it happen, it's important to know what you're willing and unwilling to do.

When we're starting out, we often say yes to everything because we're so excited. As time goes on, though, we notice that we're saying yes to too many things and it's taking a toll on our energy and ability to do things that we want to spend more time on. When this happens, we have to set nice, solid boundaries that define what we will and will not do. Your time is highly valuable and it's a privilege to spend time with you. So say no to anything that you don't want to do.

As we start to make it happen, people take notice and want a piece of the action. This is a beautiful thing. But by saying yes to *everything* by default, we're saying no to opportunities that might be beneficial to our goals. Every yes means we're automatically saying no to something else. Maybe to a better experience that hasn't presented itself yet, or perhaps to alone-time that will help recharge our batteries. When we're busy bees and "on" a lot of the time, it's crucial to get downtime too.

There are many ways to set boundaries. Here are a few to try out:

• Never say yes to something right away unless you are 110% excited about it. Tell the person asking you that you appreciate the amazing opportunity and you have to think about it. This will give you time to digest and figure out if you want to do it or not. Saying no is the same way. Don't say no unless you're absolutely certain you don't want to do it. You may as well give yourself the opportunity to think about it.

- Before you take anything on, listen for a "yes feeling" or a "no feeling" (as we talked about in chapter 5) and respond accordingly.

- Write a "fuck-it list." A TEDX speaker named Scott Jones in Vancouver introduced me to the idea of writing one of these. Rather than a bucket list, write a fuck-it list of all the things you're not going to do and then—no ifs, ands, or buts—don't do them.

- Set limits on what you'll do for other people. For example, if someone asks you to have a coffee meeting on the other side of town, tell them that although you'd love to see them, you're only available to meet at a certain location or you prefer to chat over the phone. If they think you're being a diva, then they don't have to meet with you. But if they value your time, then they'll be happy to. The key is not to be a jerk about it. When you respect your boundaries, other people have no choice but to do so too.

- Set limits on when you'll answer emails and work-related phone calls. For example, you might decide that you won't answer emails after 6 p.m. on weekdays or on weekends. I highly recommend having a set time that you finish work every day.

- Promise to do things only when you're sure you can deliver. If a store you sell your product to places a massive order and wants it shipped yesterday, tell them truthfully what you can manage. If you don't, you might risk losing them altogether. You have to be honest with yourself, first and foremost, and honour what you're capable of.

- As your business expands, assign as many of your tasks to others so that you can be free to put your best skills to work.

Boundaries are a container for your life that make it *way* easier for you to accomplish big things. Learning to set boundaries takes time, but it gets easier when you realize what you can say no to. I've dreaded saying no because I was afraid of hurting someone's feelings and then discovered it hasn't really caused any pain. Think about when a friend declines an invitation. You probably don't lose sleep over it.

Stop Working Too Much

When we're starting out, it's common to work constantly and have practically no life. If you're living this way now, please know that you're not alone. You probably don't even mind because you love what you do, and it feels good to do it a lot. In the beginning, this is totally fine and can be healthy. But at some point, you'll have to set some boundaries if you don't want to burn out and risk getting sick.

If you work constantly, you might be so out of touch with boundaries that you don't remember what they are. Also, if you own your own business, people just assume you work non-stop, so they don't expect anything less. Having fun on evenings and the weekends may not even cross your mind anymore, and as a result your friends have likely stopped calling. And you might not even notice or care because you're so wrapped up in business.

Again, at the early stages, this level of hustle can be completely warranted. But listen if your body starts talking. Its whispers might sound like getting sick more than usual or having a lot of headaches. If these symptoms worsen or become chronic, take note and set some boundaries.

I have a boundary around email. I simply don't answer work emails after 6 p.m. on weekdays or on the weekends. Sometimes I check my phone in case there's an emergency, but unless it's urgent I don't answer.

When I began running Make It, I received all exhibitor emails. There were a ton of them, especially around show season. Many were questions about little things, like the size of the table or if a chair was included. I wanted to be as efficient as possible, so I would answer each email as soon as I received it, regardless the time of day. This meant that I never really had a break from my computer or phone.

Then I learned something. If I answered those emails during business hours instead of the moment I received them, no one seemed to care. It made zero difference to them, but for me there was a huge advantage. This is an example of setting a boundary. You have to teach people what they can and can't expect from you.

Love Yourself Up

Boundaries have a lot to do with self-love. When we respect ourselves and our time, it's a hell of a lot easier to inspire others to do the same. When you run your own business, it's natural to want people to like you and think you're a competent owner. The truth is, they'll likely have more respect for you if they see you valuing yourself.

If you're running a business with a degree of customer service—and you probably are because pretty much every business does—you need to set standards for what you will and won't do. Otherwise, people might walk all over you. It won't be their intention, but it will happen whether they're conscious of it or not. Most of us want to please people, especially our customers. This is a good thing and will serve you very well long term. But be realistic about your bandwidth. If you tell a customer you can make a custom bespoke necklace in a week and you can't deliver, you'll just disappoint them.

Under-promise and over-deliver. That way, you'll have the opportunity to delight someone. The opposite is never good and will turn people off your brand. When in doubt, always be honest and impeccable with your word. People will be enticed to build a long-term relationship with you when they can trust your promises. Be firm but fair. Give what you can while preserving your integrity.

Take Charge

These guidelines apply to large and small businesses. If you employ people, train them to represent you in the way you want. If something goes wrong with your staff, it's tempting to blame them instead of shouldering the responsibility yourself. But when you're the boss, you're ultimately accountable. If an employee does something you're unhappy with, ask yourself if you trained them well and communicated clearly. If you did and something still went wrong, consider if you did a good job by hiring them. We all make mistakes, but when you're at the helm, you can't point the finger.

When you create boundaries effectively, life feels easier and simpler. A set of guidelines helps you make decisions. When you stop doing something that you've usually done in the past, it feels strange and awkward. This is to be expected. Over time, it will get easier. It's like building a muscle.

Take my experience with Make It, for example. As Make It has grown, my role as a founder has changed. In the beginning, I was extremely accessible to any Makie who needed anything. Now I have an exhibitor coordinator, so I'm less available. At first I felt weird about this, but for the company to grow and for us to be able to serve more people, my role needed to evolve. I was afraid this change would make me seem unfriendly or unapproachable, but that hasn't been the case. My team is amazing and they do many tasks better than I ever did.

Boundaries allow you the space to grow, expand, and flow. Being an effective leader is one of your fundamental skills. We often assume everyone excels at the things we're naturally good at. Understanding that you're different in the most amazing way is a massive and crucial realization. Own how awesome you are because if you don't, no one else will. When you value the gifts you've been given, everything magically shifts.

Be a Business Owner

Among the biggest challenges creative entrepreneurs face is the belief that they're not good at business and the resistance to figuring it out. Some think that they'll never be good at business, so they avoid it, hoping that if their art is good enough, someone will come along and take care of the business for them. You might think this way yourself. Chances are you *love* making your product, but the idea of getting it out into the world might be freaking scary. If you feel this way, you're definitely not alone.

To make it happen, you have to acknowledge that you're running a business. Think like an entrepreneur first and an artist second. Maybe this isn't what you want to hear, but it's the truth.

A New Take on Business

Business isn't what a lot of people think. So much changed with social media. The way messages are communicated by large brands has shifted significantly. If a marketing message isn't authentic, people see right through it immediately. We are inundated with so many messages that our processing abilities have diminished. To communicate effectively, you have to connect with people on an emotional level. Otherwise, your message will be filtered out.

Maya Angelou said, "People will forget what you said, people will forget what you did, but people will never forget how you made them feel." As human beings, we always want to feel a certain way. Ideally, we seek to feel positive, happy, and loved. Businesses exist because they give people a desired feeling.

Like a bazillion other people, I'm really attracted to Apple products. I've been a loyal user of iPhones and MacBooks for years. Whenever there's a big new product launch, I get excited, even if it's not something that I'm looking to buy. I'm not alone in this, which is why Apple is so successful all over the world. I love their products because the brand has certain characteristics that are attractive to me. The products are simple to use, functional, and aesthetically pleasing. I feel a connection to these qualities because they help me to be the person I want to be. Therefore, I feel value when I purchase an Apple product.

People choose to support brands that they feel a sense of connection with. We don't often think about what that connection is, but if we reflect on it, we can figure it out.

This is all marketing really is: the experience someone has with your brand. Customers have an experience with your brand whether you're conscious of it or not. What's exciting and terrifying (excitifying!) is that you have full control over the messages you deliver.

Marketing is telling your story in a way that people can understand and relate to. The story we tell with Make It is that craft fairs can be fun, positive, and upbeat. When you're a part of the show, you become a Makie and a sense of community and belonging goes with that. You can meet new, awesome people who share a love of selling what they make. For the customers, the story is that they can come to an event, find outstanding handmade items, and have a great time. We tell this story with the font we use on flyers, with Makie and Foxie mascots, with photos we post on Instagram, and with the Makies who sell at the show and the loyal customers who share the story with their friends. Everyone has their own experiences of Make It, hopefully positive ones, but I have no direct control over that. People decide what a story means to them because of how they interpret their observations.

Know how you tell your story, and through what channels, and tell it as best you can. Then let go of your expectations about how it will be received. You have no control over what people think of you. Do what feels good in your heart and the rest will figure itself out.

Trudy Ann Tellis of Trudy Ann's Chai & Spices (trudyannschai.com)

Trudy Ann is one of those people who immediately make an impression. She's warm, enthusiastic, and has fascinating stories to share. She's been a Makie since 2010. She's also a reiki master who sees the world in a unique and magical way. Her chai business was developed by following up on wisdom she gained from listening to universal impulses and by following traditions and rituals cultivated in India.

Trudy Ann was born in Bombay (now called Mumbai) and spent every summer at her family's home in Mangalore. As a small child, she loved skipping through the garden and helping her great-aunt Mary pick aboli flowers to string into garlands and sell on the street. This great introduction to entrepreneurship helped Trudy Ann earn some pocket money too.

When she was a little bit older, she teamed up with her brother Glen to resell peanuts they found in Mary's pantry, along with green mangos they picked from the trees in her back yard. Although Glen was the mastermind behind this venture, Trudy Ann was hooked. She has fond memories of watching her aunty collect fresh ingredients from the market and grind them up with a mortar and pestle before combining them in a pot on a wood-burning stove. The aroma was intoxicating and one that left an impression.

From the ages of 13 to 20, Trudy Ann worked alongside Mother Teresa, helping to care for sick and dying people at a care facility called Asha Daan, where she worked with disabled children. Although it could be physically challenging, her profound experience with Mother Teresa moulded Trudy Ann into who she is today and ignited her passion for helping the less fortunate. One special evening, while everyone else was sleeping, she had the opportunity to pray with Mother Teresa alone.

In 1987, Trudy Ann to moved to Upstate New York to attend college, where she specialized in inclusive education for children with autism. After that, she moved to the San Francisco Bay Area to be a special education teacher. She eventually met her husband, had two sons, and in 2003, when the boys were three and seven, she took her family to India for a year so that they could learn about their culture.

Trudy Ann wanted to spend as much time at home with her children as she could rather than continuing to teach. Based on a strong impulse, she moved to Vancouver because she knew it was the place for her to go next. A year later, the family settled into a home just off Commercial Drive.

Trudy Ann had always loved making chai, and some of her friends in San Francisco had already told her she should open a café. But it was her son's saxophone teacher asking her how much she would charge for a bag of chai that prompted her to get serious about selling her spice mixes.

A major obstacle that had held Trudy Ann back from starting a business was seizures. After doing a few small craft fairs in 2009 and in 2010, she participated at her first Make It show in Vancouver, at the Croatian Cultural Centre. Although it was a big success and she almost sold out of chai, she knew that to continue to participate at larger shows, she needed to solve her challenging heath problem. In 2012, Trudy Ann underwent brain surgery and has been seizure-free ever since!

After fully recovering from brain surgery, Trudy Ann dived into her business and continued selling at craft fairs, farmers' markets, online, and to stores. At first, she was doing everything herself, but slowly over the years she has hired staff to help her package and sell. But Trudy Ann will never let go of blending the spices for her chai. It's her secret formula that makes Trudy Ann's Chai & Spices special and unique. In the early days, she folded all the little tea envelopes herself, just like she did for the ones that held the peanuts she sold as a kid, but now she knows the importance of concentrating her efforts where her business is best served.

In 2016, Trudy Ann released a cookbook that tells her story of growing up in India and shares family recipes. Her line of chai and spices is expanding, and she now sells at craft fairs across the country, including at all the Make It shows. Her teas and spices are even sold in Whole Foods! She has many new, exciting ideas in the works, for instance taking tour groups to India to show them her mystical home through her eyes. She's passionate about helping people to heal through nutrition and she has a wealth of knowledge about what to eat and what to avoid.

Trudy Ann's passion, drive, and positivity set her apart from many of her peers. These resources come from her daily meditation, her nutritious diet, and her openly giving and receiving love. At Make It, many of the Makies stop by her booth to receive short reiki sessions that boost up their vibes. At the shows, Trudy Ann serves up chai samples, grooves in her booth whenever a song she likes comes on, and radiates joy all around. She takes a lot of pride in her booth at Make It, and because her customers can feel that, it comes back to her in fantastic sales.

Here are Trudy Ann's tips for making it happen:

- Envision something *big* from the beginning.

- Always listen to your customers. Talk to them and ask them questions about what they would most like to see from you.

- Share your own story and be open to hearing others. You never know the difference that might make in someone's life.

- If you encounter negativity, kill it with kindness and if that doesn't work, block that low-vibe energy from coming back to you.

- Keep your judgement in your pockets. Trudy Ann's favourite Mother Teresa quote is "If you judge people, you have no time to love them."

- Remember the people who were with you from the beginning and don't compromise to make a quick buck.

- If something doesn't work, cut your losses and drop it.

- To set an appropriate price, know your costs. Make peace with numbers so they don't scare you.

- Listen, and follow the impulses that you receive. There is a reason for them.

- Treat your staff like family and your body like a temple. They will both be with you for a long time.

- Once you decide something, you *do it*!

Be Helpable

Not many artists and makers take advantage of the power of community. A huge network of people currently living their dreams is out there. They've walked the walk and have learned a ton along the way. Get to know them and tap into their knowledge. This can expedite your learning curve and save you time, money, and effort.

The concepts that follow can feel pretty uncomfortable, especially if you're introverted or shy. I promise you that all the amazing rewards that come from taking these steps will make the awkward feelings worthwhile. Plus, like most things, doing them is never as bad as you imagine them to be.

Find Mentors and Role Models

When I started Booty Beltz, I didn't have a clue what I was doing. I was very young, had no experience and no idea where to begin. Luckily, I pursued role models who appeared to be killing it. Some I had the privilege to meet in person, and others I admired from afar. Doubtlessly, finding mentors was among the most beneficial things I did.

I sought out mentors who were young women, a little bit older than me but who appeared to have figured it all out—at least it seemed that way from their websites! They were selling in tons of stores, got constant press, and had celebrities wearing their designs. Plus, they seemed like awesome ladies that I would want as friends. This is an important thing to look for in a mentor, along with an alignment in your aesthetics, brand personality, and customer demographic. If you think you could be friends with them, there's a better chance for a real connection.

Once I zeroed in on a potential mentor, I would online stalk them to learn as much information about them as I could. This sounds a bit creepy, but with all the information available online it's pretty simple to do. I would take a close look at where they were selling, how they were marketing, what their price point was, and anything else I could use to better my business savvy.

I would go to the stores they sold to in my area and check out how their product was displayed, what point-of-sales they used, and how everything was packaged. I would talk to the store buyer or a clerk to figure out how the product was selling and ask about the designers. I discovered *so* much information this way that I found many shortcuts and saved a bunch of time. When the moment was right, I reached out to my mentors, and if they lived in the same city, I politely asked if I could buy them lunch and hear more about their story.

The Exchange

In asking someone you admire to meet with you, be helpable and offer them something in return. I can't count how many people email me because they "want to go for coffee and pick my brain." Ugh. Don't ever ask that. Who the heck wants their brain picked? It doesn't exactly sound pleasant or enticing. And coffee? At least offer to buy lunch!

What you have to give might not be obvious. You might think your mentor's living the life, so how could you offer anything of value? This is a limiting belief that can be reversed. Like all successful relationships, the one with your mentor should be a balance of give and take.

Just because you might be new to the business game doesn't mean you're lacking in awesome skills. Maybe you're a yoga instructor who could offer a few free classes. You might have a background in graphic design and could create a new flyer. If you're looking for help, a good rule of thumb is to offer something of value in return. Your mentor might never take you up on it, but she will be touched and appreciative because you're thinking of her. Graciousness and generosity are usually appreciated. Plus, when people feel good, they're even more motivated to help you.

Build a long-term relationship. A time will likely come when you're able to offer your mentor some guidance. This will be a keystone moment when the student becomes the teacher. Generosity is important in building a strong connection, so give any time you can.

Ask for Specifics

Reach out with a specific question or request for help. If you go in too vague, your mentor won't know what you really need and, since they're busy, likely won't have the time or energy to find out. Be clear and concise with your ask. For example, if you need more media coverage for your business but don't know where to begin, you could ask about press releases. Maybe your mentor has one they've used in the past and would be willing to show it to you or give you some of their media contacts. But don't take offence if they say no to a request. Your mentors might not be willing to share everything. So that it's not uncomfortable for either of you, preface any big ask by saying that you understand they may not be able to meet it.

There's no point reinventing the wheel. When you have people in your life who you look up to and who help you on your path, things are a lot simpler. You might want mentors in different industries or modalities too. If you're a jeweller, for instance, your mentor could be someone who makes gorgeous pottery. Even if your mentor lives in a different city or country, there are plenty of ways to communicate.

Your prospective mentor might not be interested in helping you. This might feel harsh, but you don't need to take it personally or let it get you down. They could have countless reasons that you'll never know about. Plus, even if they don't want to engage with you one on one, you can learn from their online presence.

I love to pay it forward and help others make a living doing what they love. I was inspired to write this book because I want to help as many people as I can. As the old saying goes, nobody is an island. Every successful person has been helped by someone along the way.

You're Not Alone

You don't have to make it happen alone, nor should you. Entrepreneurial folks have a certain traits that makes them more resistant to seeking help. Maybe it's because we don't want to admit we need it or we don't think anyone can help us. Regardless, it's silly, so stop it!

Recently, I found a diary from when I was in my mid 20s. Reading about what I was going through at that time broke my heart a little bit. Young Jenna had to break through so many barriers, and some of those days were so painful. Although I had reached out to mentors and had a lot of support, often I felt lonely and isolated. It was understandably difficult for my friends to know what I was going through when I started Booty Beltz. They weren't developing a business straight out of university like I was. I also didn't have access to any role models in my immediate community. At times, I felt like I just couldn't go on, like no one truly understood what I was going through. Oh, the anguish!

Seeing someone else do what we want to do gives us permission to dream big too. If they could do it, it has to be possible for us. Knowing our role models have bad days just like we do eases the burden somewhat. So, in hard times, remember that even if your journey is completely different from mine, I'm living proof that you can make your dreams come true. The more role models we have, the easier it is to accomplish our dreams.

Be Gentle with Yourself

Would you speak to an innocent child the way you do to yourself? If your answer is, "Hell no!" then you should reconsider your self-talk. Yelling at yourself like a drill sergeant isn't empowering or inspiring. How is scolding ourselves to do better helpful? It isn't. Discipline is necessary to achieve results, but there's a more loving way. You can speak to yourself in a kind and gentle tone and remind yourself of all the awesome things you've already achieved.

I've only had a couple of bosses in my life because, as you know, I started my entrepreneurial journey at a very young age. But if I had a kind, sweet, awesome boss who encouraged me, I would be a lot more productive than if I answered to a tyrant. When you talk to yourself, be the type of boss you'd choose to answer to.

Stop Editing

While creating, you access part of the brain that needs to run free and unchecked. It's the part of your brain that allows you to dance like nobody's watching, sing like no one can hear, and fully show up and be yourself. It's the magic spot where you're in free flow and accessing a state of being that creates at the highest possible level. This is full-blown inspired co-creation, baby! It doesn't happen a lot, but when it does, there's nothing else like it.

The problem is, this state doesn't strike at a chosen moment. You have to wait for the muse to come when she wants. It's like waiting for a wave while surfing. You can't force it with your mind. You have to allow it to happen. Sometimes you have to be patient for a very long time, and sometimes it just happens all of a sudden before you feel ready.

Inspiration swoops in and lifts your wings so you can finally fly. You've been ready and waiting, showing up and doing the work. Now it's time for the magic to take over and elevate you to that next level. You can sometimes tell when someone's going through this because suddenly their social media becomes more interesting. They're going to fabulous places, getting publicity for their accomplishments, meeting cool people. It's a point of liftoff and they're living proof that the next level is possible.

Kids readily share their talents and creativity. They're encouraged to be this way. Then, somewhere along the line, someone criticizes them—it could be the word of an unknowing parent or a bully at school—and they shrink a little bit. All the same, it hurts. The craziest thing is that, as adults, we're not conscious of many of these past wounds.

When we hear a negative voice creeping up and making us feel guilty for not doing enough or having achieved enough, we must instead affirm that we've already done more than most people, and that our community is grateful and appreciative of our service. In other words, look for the evidence that proves you're on the right path.

The Spirituality of Success

Success is a spiritual journey. Many of us never truly feel successful because we haven't understood what this means. I was into spiritual practices at a young age and felt I had a good understanding of the laws of the Universe, but still, I thought success was something you had to strive toward. No matter how hard I worked, though, I never felt like

I arrived. All indications could show me that I had, but I didn't feel it inside myself. It was frustrating, sad, and lonely.

Success is something that must be felt in the moment because the present is all we have. If we don't feel success now, we'll never feel it. Often when we hit the target, an anticlimactic, low feeling sets in. We think, *Now what?* But we can train ourselves to be in the moment and have gratitude and appreciation for our creations.

No One Knows Better Than You

The most spiritual person in the world doesn't know any better than you do. All they have is different awareness and experience. No one knows what's best for you or what you should do next. Your life choices are up to you, which is a dynamic feeling. No one is going to move forward for you nor are they going to tell you how to do it. Very excitifying!

When you take full responsibility for your life, it shifts. If we reflect deeply on areas of our lives that aren't working well, we often notice that we're subconsciously blaming other people for our own shortcomings. For instance, a lot of people blame their parents for how they've turned out. None of us gets to pick our parents, and I don't think there's a family out there that's perfect, even the ones that look perfect from the outside. It's the grit of childhood that shapes and builds our character. Whatever your parents did wrong while raising you, they also did a lot of things right. If they didn't, you wouldn't be here now reading this book. When we let go of blaming others for the circumstances of our lives, we become powerful and autonomous. We become the architects designing the blueprint of our lives.

Let the Spirit Lift You

You've probably experienced that delightful feeling of being in the zone and time standing still. After eight hours of work, you realize that you've eaten only a granola bar all day! When you're working from this place, anything is possible. You can't help but feel the magic of how good it is to be here. This is your genius zone and in it procrastination doesn't stand a chance. You've let passion, which is a much higher vibration, run the show. Expand these good feelings for as long as possible.

If I feel happy because I learn that a newspaper is writing an article about Make It, I might do a dance of joy and sing a silly little song to extend my elation. At first, this might feel awkward, but after a few attempts it will feel authentic and those good vibes last longer. Extend your good vibes the same way you might eat a delectable piece of cake. Rather than inhaling it in a couple of massive bites, savour each piece in your mouth slowly and deliberately.

When you're in the flow, the floodgates open and things manifest all around you. This is true for creative projects like it is for dating. It's usually when you're on top of the world that the cute guy messages, asking you out on a date. Maybe you get a cheque you weren't expecting in the mail too. Good vibes attract more good vibes, so you might as well milk them for all they're worth.

The more you allow positive experiences to be attracted to you, the more they'll come. You open to the flow and natural abundance shows up. What you have to be aware of is actively receiving these new realities and not self-sabotaging because you don't feel like you're worthy.

You can decide what you're worthy of. When you look at other people who have the sort of success that you desire, do you ever wonder what they're doing differently? Do they have a special skill or ritual that they practise? Maybe they do, and definitely they have a belief system that supports their reality. If they didn't, they wouldn't be able to maintain it.

Many people fail to make it happen because they don't know how to make the leap. They could be smart and hard-working, but there's another factor at play that goes beyond those two skills. Faith is everything. Certain realities can't be argued. If you jump up, gravity will pull you back to Earth. If you harness the power and energy of positive thought, you'll reap the rewards for what you put into the world.

Grace

I love the word *grace*. It makes me think of effortlessness and elegance. It's a feminine energy word that suggests letting go and trusting all will be good in the world. It's not forcing or manipulating. It's allowing for something greater than yourself to take the wheel.

If you're like me, you love the idea of letting go and allowing another force of energy to step in, but you find it difficult to trust that it actually will. What if it doesn't and you waste a bunch of time, money, and energy? The hard part is, if you doubt it, it's unlikely that you'll receive its boost. The energy of distrust blocks the thing you want so badly. *Ugh!* This can be frustrating, but isn't it also pretty magical and amazing?

At a certain point while writing this book, I felt like my fingers had little brains of their own and they'd glide across my keyboard effortlessly. I didn't have to force anything or overthink it, I just opened myself up and let it flow. If you reflect on your own life, you'll likely recall having similar experiences of ease. An open, relaxed, playful, and joyful mindset is a portal for grace. In such a state, things have a way of flowing in.

Travelling might open you up to grace too. There are certain places in the world where I feel unstoppable and seem to be a magnet for creative energy. New York and Bali are two very different places, but both fill my soul like nowhere else. I'm my best when I'm in these places, and grace can permeate my life very easily.

The people and information that we expose ourselves to can also inspire grace. You likely have people who light you up because every time you hang out with them you feel better afterward. Maybe they inspire a different part of your brain and you come up with the best ideas when you're around them.

I call certain people in my life my magical unicorn friends. They're inspiring, positive, fun, and they bring out the best version of me. Even if it's been a long time since we've seen each other, there's kismet and serendipity when we meet. If something feels off, we talk about it so that it doesn't turn into a thing. It's important to choose people whose presence, like yours, allows for grace to flow through your experiences together.

Make It Real

Some of the exercises in this chapter may feel like a stretch, but trust me, you're working new muscles and doing so will serve to strengthen you.

1.   Commit to strengthening your boundaries. Make a deal with yourself that for the next week, whenever you're

asked to do something, tell the person making the request that you need a day or two to decide on your answer. Take this time to arrive at a decision aligned with your truth.

2. Make a fuck-it list. As a way of setting boundaries around your time and the energy you give to things that don't support your dreams, make a list of all the things you're no longer going to do. Praise and recognize yourself when you follow through on your commitment to not doing.

3. For 20 minutes, pay close attention to how you speak to yourself. If you catch yourself being harsh, recalibrate to a positive, caring voice. For more insight, practise this for longer periods of time.

4. The next time you have a win and are feeling great, do something to extend the joy (for example, dance, sing, draw, run, laugh with friends). Cultivate the good feelings by keeping them going. In your journal, write about how this felt. Use descriptive language so that you capture as much depth and detail about your experience as possible.

nine

The Magic after You Make It Happen

"Never let life impede on your ability to
manifest your dreams. Dig deeper into your dreams
and deeper into yourself and believe that anything
is possible, and make it happen."

CORIN NEMEC

As we come to the end of our make it happen journey, we can look back and see how far we've travelled,
all the obstacles we've overcome to get to this special
place. We can look ahead to the next big thing. But—most
importantly—we can celebrate our moments of success.
When you make it happen, the Universe gives you special
superpowers. It's like getting invited to a VIP club that only
other people making it happen can access. There's a vibe
that you automatically give off when you reach a milestone.
Maybe it's the swagger in your step, the sparkle in your eye,
or the confidence in your smile. Whatever it is for you, my

biggest hope and dream is that you see it when you look at your gorgeous face in the mirror.

The Power of Finishing

There's a whole lot of power in finishing what you set out to do. Nothing feels better than being done. Not only can you relish accomplishing something that will impact the world in positive ways, but you can close a chapter in your mind and open up bandwidth for more awesome things.

At the end of the Make It shows, we take a Makie family photo. This tradition started on a whim in 2013. Now we do it to celebrate each and every show. It's pretty phenomenal to see all the Makies gather around and celebrate themselves and one another for accomplishing something big. Not everyone participates, but those who do get a lot out of it because it symbolizes something special. For me, the moment completes a cycle and a big wave of relief passes over me. Even though there's more work to come and I'm exhausted, I stay present so that I can revel in and soak up the magnificence of finishing. It's a beautiful state and I'm grateful to experience it multiple times a year.

The prospect of being done is a powerful feeling that can drive us to sprint to the finish line. When you pass the point of no return on your make it happen journey, you'll need this fuel to stop anything from holding you back. When you complete what you set out to do, there's no one who can take that away from you. It's a spectacular feeling. Soak in its glory for as long as you possibly can.

One of the most devastating things we can do is quit when the finish line is in sight. Sometimes, when people see that what they truly want is right in front of them, fear takes over, making them do crazy shit to sabotage their project. Whatever you do, don't let this be you! Why climb to the top of the mountain and then not enjoy the view? You deserve to be there, savouring it for everything it's worth.

Keep going until you experience the glory of completion. When you cross a finish line once, you know you can do it again. This must be why so many people run multiple marathons. After completing any worthy pursuit, you step up a level on the spiral staircase.

A Bittersweet Victory

Making it happen can be bittersweet. The high of completion is followed shortly thereafter by the question, *Now what?* When Make It ends, I'm always in a weird headspace for a few days. Immediately after the show, I feel like I'm on cloud nine. After we pack up, I go out for a celebratory dinner with my team or with Chandler. We order drinks and toast the show. Although I'm exhausted, I usually have a hard time sleeping that night because I'm so amped up on adrenaline.

But I wake up the next morning to mixed emotions from being overly tired and relieved while simultaneously wondering if I did okay. Despite the success of the show, a tiny part of me wonders if I did a good enough job and if people are happy. There will likely never be a time in my life when I'm 100% satisfied with what I've accomplished. But I can recognize this natural human tendency, love myself up a little more, and then release my inner critic from doing its job.

We're all hard on ourselves. I have many fabulous entrepreneurial friends who are rocking it, but deep down they also feel this way. A nagging voice persists in asking if there was more that could have been done. Accept this for what it is and then let it go. No matter how high you get, it's always possible to go higher. The journey is never over or fully complete.

Finishing Make It feels like slamming on the breaks while driving a race car. When you hustle to get something done for any length of time, you adapt to living at that speed. If you don't slow down once in a while, you'll burn out and lose everything you've been working so hard to achieve. Check in with yourself regularly to make sure that you're doing okay, otherwise you run the risk of burnout.

Slowing down can feel anticlimactic. This doesn't have anything to do with your level of success. It's just weird to change speeds quickly. I've felt this way many times over, as have friends of mine who produce events, music, films, and other creative projects. We feel a bit sad and depressed, despite knowing that we "should" be proud and want to celebrate. People on the outside assume that because you're done, you're nothing but satisfied and full of relief. When I explain how I'm feeling to friends and family who don't do this kind of work, most of them look at me like I'm kind of crazy!

Another Step on the Spiral Staircase

In chapter 6, we talked about the spiral staircase as a metaphor for the make it happen journey. When you're finished your project you're at Step 11, which means you go back to Step 1 but—this time—on a new level. You've done things that can be leveraged to help get to your next destination faster.

I've been organizing craft fairs since 2007, and I begin each show's cycle in a similar way. Because I've been doing it for so long, I have better systems in place than when I started, and I do the show from a new level of the staircase each time. When writing this book, I started at ground level, the very bottom, because I'd never written a book before and didn't know what I was doing. Now I have a better understanding of how the process unfolds. The next book will be a heck of a lot easier too, because I'll have done one loop around the staircase.

CASE STUDY
Jennifer Wilson of VONBON
(vonbon.ca)
· · · · · · · · · · · · ·

The founder of VONBON, Jennifer Wilson, is a remarkable entrepreneur who's built an exceptional business in a short amount of time. Not only is she a fierce lady boss, but she's also a mother of two young children. She's been at many levels of the spiral staircase on her journey, sometimes on more than one step at once. Plus, Jen has a huge social media following. To top it off, she's gorgeous and sweet. Her story serves as an inspiration for how we can keep making it happen in bigger and better ways.

VONBON started as a happy accident in April 2013. Jen was at the age when a bunch of her friends were starting families, and she struggled to find hip, stylish, eco-friendly clothing to give them as shower gifts. At that time, all the conscious fabrics were either brown, grey, or moss green and weren't all that cute. She didn't have much experience with design, but she thought she could do better, which prompted her to start designing her own fabric.

Jen was working full time as a dental hygienist. She loved her job because it allowed her to connect with people, but she found all the bending over and repetitive motions difficult on her body. When she told a patient about her baby clothing idea, she excitedly let Jen know she had a connection with a prominent Vancouver blogger named Monika Hibbs. The patient offered to send Monika some samples of Jen's work.

That was the beginning of her wild and crazy entrepreneurial adventure. Monika *loved* Jen's prototypes and featured them on her Instagram. People immediately asked about ordering them. Jen hadn't officially launched her business, but this twist of fate forced her to move fast. She decided on the name VONBON because she and her husband had planned to name their future son (should they have a boy) Von, and Vonbon was to be his cute nickname.

Another serendipitous event occurred in April 2013. Jen was at Make It Vancouver visiting her cousin Mindan, who's a loyal Makie. As she was leaving the show, Jen noticed a Make It University flyer on a table. She grabbed it and enrolled in my online business program. I still remember receiving her excited emails about her progress. I'm honoured that she feels I created something valuable and that it allowed her to gain the clarity she needed to start VONBON.

Jen became a very busy lady. She inherited a strong work ethic from her parents, who are also entrepreneurs. When VONBON was starting out, she used her lunch hours at the dental office to answer emails and post on Instagram and dedicated her evenings to shipping orders. At first, she didn't have a website but scrambled to launch one. Luckily, she has two very supportive sisters, who helped her get everything together. Even with the help, she quickly felt burnt out.

To keep up with demand, Jen reduced her work to part time hours so that she could fulfill all the orders that came from her popular Instagram feed. She loves Instagram and knows it's a big part of why VONBON grew so quickly. With Mindan's encouragement, Jen signed up for Make It only six months after launching VONBON. Her goal was to do $10,000 in sales, which she got quite close to. That's pretty phenomenal for someone so new to the game.

After Make It, Jen realized what a viable business VONBON was. So she took a leap of faith and quit her job. She also became pregnant with her first child. Reflecting back, she really doesn't know how she was able to do it all, but somehow she did.

The second bedroom of her home had become VONBON's headquarters, but with a baby on the way she had to move the office. Having the business in her home was also hard on her marriage because she worked around the clock to keep up. She took an office in Yaletown and hired some support staff to fulfill online orders.

Now VONBON runs out of a beautiful showroom and Jen has two full-time staff as well as many subcontractors. She also finally had a son named Von, but his nickname isn't Vonbon because, she said, that would be weird! Jen continues to be extremely active on social media and it's the number one way new customers find her. On Instagram, she frequently posts stories that engage her customers. Although this takes a lot of energy, it allows her to connect with moms who are inspired by her.

Jen is living proof that a busy mom can make it happen. She's generous in sharing her story with adoring fans and extremely savvy when it comes to connecting with influencers. Whatever your views on social media, Jen is working it for all it's worth and it's paying off big time.

What people love most about VONBON is the quality of the fabric and her designs. She has an eye for style that's reflected in her line. Because demand continues to grow, Jen is considering a trip to Asia to see if it's possible to have VONBON produced overseas. She's torn about this decision because of her handmade roots but also has to be realistic about the potential of her fast-growing brand. What I know about Jen is that, because of her strong work ethic and ambitious nature, she'll have nothing but massive success in the future.

The VONBON story is proof that when you get out of your own way, sensational things can happen. Listening to the subtle cues from the Universe and following your instincts is the way to go. Jen has done an outstanding job of surrounding herself with a supportive community that wants to see her thrive, which is exactly what she's doing.

Here are Jen's best tips for making it happen:

• Your connection to your customers is your number one business asset. Value them and they will value you.

- Always trust your gut and take the leap before you're ready.

- No one is totally well-rounded. Know what you're outstanding at and hire other people to do the rest.

- Don't wait until it's perfect or for all your ducks to be in a row. Just start!

- When you have a hot product, people will replicate it. Don't waste your energy trying to take them out, just look ahead and focus on what's next. If they're copying you, they can only do what you've already done.

- When you're super-active on social media, it's important to have solid boundaries and balance. This is especially true when you have a family.

- People are buying more than what you're selling. They're buying you, but only if you're genuine and authentic in everything you do.

- When people love what you're doing, they'll want to share it.

Dream a Bigger Dream

The only way to have a full experience in life is to be consciousness of the moment you're in. When you make it happen, the pinnacle of the experience is feeling the full expression of the moment. Fully experience the moment by:

- Feeling the success in the cells of your body.

- Recognizing and appreciating what you've created.
- Then moving on to dream a bigger dream.

Being a visionary means your vision always evolves and grows. The first Make It show was small, with about 30 exhibitors. I was so worried that no one would show up that I went door to door and dropped flyers in mailboxes. My dream was simply to draw customers so that the exhibitors wouldn't think the show was a disaster and regret that they signed up for it. Overall, I could tell the show was a success because the people who participated wanted to come back for more. Some of those first Makies are still part of Make It today. And they've expanded their dreams to accomplish their goals as well.

Dreams are usually seen as positive, uplifting, and beautiful. But if you get too attached to them or don't dream big enough, they lead you astray. Dreaming is always best done at your highest vibrational state (when you're feeling joyous, positive, free, grateful). When you are vibing high, you can envision things more clearly. It's like tuning in to a radio station when its signal is strong. You just get there a lot easier and faster. If you try to dream when you're feeling down, it'll be difficult and take much longer to hit the spot, if you get there at all.

Dreams are intentional thoughts about what your life at a higher vibration could look like. If you see it in your mind, you can be it in your life! The only thing stopping you is all the limitations you put in your way.

Even when we visualize a dream, the Universe may have a grander plan for us. When I started out on my entrepreneurial journey in 2003, I did not envision the exact dream

I'm living today. I knew I wanted to have a big, full, adventurous life doing the work I love, but I wasn't overly specific. I allowed serendipitous moments to carry me along, without getting too caught up in what the path was supposed to look like. Some experiences have been tremendous, and some have been awful. But every day I learn something new about myself and how the Universe works. Trust and surrender to the flow and you'll go places you could never imagine.

Now one of my dreams is to get married to my soulmate and have children. I haven't met him yet, but I know it's only a matter of time. Who knows, by the time you're reading, this I might very well have. On top of that, I might be a mother. I'm not hung up on the timing of these things, because I already feel in my heart that they'll happen. It's just a matter of time before these things show up in my life. I've dated a lot over the years, but I made a vow to myself never to settle for anyone who doesn't inspire me to be the best version of myself.

True love goes beyond our thoughts and can be felt but not always logically explained. Dreams of making anything happen are the same way. It's possible to see them so clearly, but until you're there and truly feel it with your entire being, you'll never know what it's like exactly. When you believe it, only then can you see it. I recently watched the movie *The Matrix* and if you haven't seen it recently, or at all, I recommend you do the same. It provides such a clear example of the power of belief. All you have to do now is make sure there's nothing in your belief system blocking what you want from showing up. Step onto the spiral staircase and surrender to the flow as you manifest your next big dream.

Rest and Recalibrate

Rest and recalibration are things that most of us need to focus on but rarely do. With smartphones, it's easy to be distracted for 99% of life. We usually have a screen in front of our faces. It's so sad to watch a crowd at a fireworks show and see most people experiencing the spectacle from behind a screen. You can't fully be present in the moment if you have a little screen in front of your face.

I've become really strict about not taking my phone into the bedroom. Buy an old-school alarm clock (yes, they still make them!) so you don't have to rely on your phone. There's an energetic difference when we keep the phone out of the room where we sleep. Another thing I've consciously worked on is my addiction to scrolling through countless photos. Some people think that surfing social media is relaxing. But it doesn't allow you the profound, nurturing rest you need for recovery after making it happen. Your body, mind, and soul need a deeper rest that's more connected to the source of your power and energy. Real self-care fulfills and energizes you to continue up the spiral staircase. Savasana is at the end of yoga classes so that your body can incorporate and integrate the benefits of the practice. Resting after making it happen operates on the same principle.

When you constantly *do* without any intentional rest, the benefits of your growth don't get incorporated into your soul. Spend time in stillness—not watching TV, reading books, playing on your phone—literally do nothing. On Instagram, I posted an image of a float tank with a caption that said, "This is where I'm writing my book." Many of the ideas you've been reading came to me while I was in the stillness of a float tank. Sensory deprivation isn't for everyone, but I find the benefits of floating are outstanding. There's nothing better than sinking into a tank and allowing my brain to open up and the flow of universal thought to enter. Much of what I know has come from opening to receiving it. I've never felt creative, inspired, or alive after wasting time on Facebook! To get the rest you need after making it happen, go on a detox. And by this, I mean cutting out the crap that you consume with your mouth, eyes, and ears.

Rest is all about listening to your body and giving it the things it needs, when it needs them. If you're tired, take a nap. If you're hungry, eat some healthy food. If you want to dance, turn on some music and shake what your mama gave you. There are no rules about self-care except to love yourself up and be gentle and kind. Don't overthink it. People relax and recharge in all sorts of ways. I'm a sucker for a great yoga class, a healthy vegetarian meal, and a massage.

Be intentional about your rest. If I set aside time to rest and don't have a plan, I end up spinning my wheels. Then, when the free time is up, I don't feel any benefit because I didn't intentionally relax. Instead, I'm more anxious and restless, which totally defeats the purpose.

Leverage What You Made Happen

The power and velocity in the space between completing one project and starting another is your leverage point. As physics has taught us, something in motion will stay in motion. You might as well use this to your advantage. The more you make amazing things happen, the faster you can zoom up that spiral staircase with grace and ease. So much of what I've already created through Make It will help me market and promote this book. When I write another book,

I'll leverage the success of this one for the next round of publicity and promotion. Everything you do works in conjunction with everything you've already done. The more magic you make happen, the more it will continue to happen and the easier it gets. Isn't that fascinating?

It's important to have intentions for everything you do. After you've made it happen, take the time to rise up and observe from a higher level, with greater perspective and appreciation, all that you've achieved. Take stock of everything you've learned, the people you've met, as well as the wins and the losses you've had. When you fully see what you've created from a bird's eye view, you'll garner a new understanding of just how powerful you are.

Love, Gratitude, and Appreciation

Without love, gratitude, and appreciation, you have nothing. These are the most important emotions we can feel. If you make it happen and you don't appreciate what you currently have, you simply won't attract what you want. When I'm fully grateful for what I have in my life right now, without judgement, then all the things I desire magically are attracted to me. I'm not exactly sure how this works, but it's miraculous so I just accept it and allow it to happen.

Everything you've accomplished in this moment is exactly what it should be. You might be shocked at the difference between what you'd imagined and how the end result looks, but my advice is to appreciate the shit out of it! I find failure an odd idea sometimes, because no matter what results you get, success *and* failure will always contain valuable lessons and insight.

Release

You are not the work you create. Sure, you made it happen and brought it into tangible form, but now that it's here you're no longer fully responsible for it. Often when you birth an idea, you feel like it's your baby, but it's not. Once you breathe life into your work it becomes independent of you and has a life of its own. If you don't release what you manifest, it becomes clingy, takes too much of your time and energy. After Make It, I can't be *too* concerned about what everyone thought of the show because I would go insane. It matters most to me what I think and experience. Please make it the same way for you and your creation.

When you release what you've made happen, don't put too much weight on how people respond to it. If you reach a lot of people, some will like it and others won't no matter how much blood, sweat, and tears went into it. Focus on how you feel about what you did. You can learn from others' criticism but listen *only* to people you love, respect, and value. As they say, haters be hatin': if you get caught up in their negativity it will only bring you down.

Throw Your Own Confetti!

Take your celebration seriously and plan for something worthy of what you've accomplished. I've been with you along this journey and I'm so proud of what you've done. You deserve wholehearted recognition. Don't half-ass your celebration because you'll never get the same opportunity to experience the glow of making happen this particular thing that you've been dreaming of for a long time. It's a sacred, deeply special moment, so give it the love and care it deserves. Throw your own confetti:

- Be completely self-indulgent.
- Don't worry about what other people think or expect.
- Only do what feels amazing to you.

This is your celebration and it doesn't matter how glamorous or impressive it looks from the outside. You're doing it for yourself, so receive and connect to the experience. Tony Robbins says success without fulfillment is the ultimate failure. When you make it happen and don't celebrate your success, it's a very unfortunate loss.

No one can celebrate your success for you. No one will take the photos or remember the important milestones if you don't. Even if you have a staff, it's up to you to decide to have the party and hire the photographer if you want to celebrate in that way. The beauty of throwing your own confetti is that you get to call the shots. Get the photo, take the video, and create your own media archive that will serve you in the future. Don't end up feeling regret for neglecting to capture the moments on your make it happen journey.

It's like when you're celebrating your birthday. Some years you might want a big party with all your friends and other years you might want to go on a solo trip. Celebrate in a way that makes you feel most alive.

The year 2016 was a big one for me. I bought my brother out of Make It and ran four shows solo, with my amazing subcontractors Brigitte and Diana. At the start of the year, I'd made a vision board and on it was a big gold star covered with diamonds. I put it on my board because it was so bright and sparkly. One afternoon, I was in Yaletown with a friend and I spotted a ring that looked almost identical to that sparkly star. I absolutely fell in love with it and tried it on. I told myself that one day the man of my dreams would buy it for me. Throughout the year, when I was in the area, I went to the store to visit my ring.

After the holiday Make It show, I was out for lunch with a friend, feeling completely exhausted and burnt out. My friend wisely asked me what I was going to do to celebrate my accomplishment. Without missing a beat, I told her I was going to go buy the sparkly star ring.

Right after lunch, I marched into the store, pointed at the ring, and told the woman working there I was going to take it. She was a little caught off guard because I was so confident and quick in my decision to buy an expensive piece of jewellery. To my delight, the price had been reduced by a nice chunk too. When I asked her if this ring had been a big seller, she told me that many women loved it and had tried it on, but no one had purchased it. The ring I was about to buy was the only one of its kind that they'd had all along. She said that she knew it was waiting for someone special, and that was me! Every day I look at my sparkly star ring and see it as my own little burst of confetti.

Don't pile on the pressure to celebrate. Just do what feels good and natural. It's all about how it feels, not how it looks. We live in an era when people are more concerned about taking beautiful photos of their food than they are about the food itself. Celebrate the important milestones by doing something uniquely special for yourself.

If you celebrate with people who have been with you on your journey, the experience may be heightened. Allow yourself to be celebrated and take in the acknowledgement of making it happen. It's a sweet, sweet feeling that *no one* can take away from you. When you accomplish what you set out to do, it's the best feeling in the world. Not only do you feel fully alive, but you also realize that you can make it happen over and over again.

Make It Real

Take the time to savour anything you've made happen. If you've been working on a big goal and that prompted you to read this book, congratulations! Write about that. If you're still working on your goal, choose another journey to reflect on. Wherever you're at, learning to relish your accomplishments will serve you.

1. Journal about all the things that you've learned along your path and that you're grateful for. They can be significant or seemingly small. Let a stream of consciousness pour out of you as you fill up with all the juicy goodness of being a truly grateful and blessed person.

2. Dream a bigger dream. Give yourself as much time as you need to fully flesh out a 1-year, 3-year, and 10-year vision for your life. Be comprehensive and cover all areas, including health, spirituality, family and friends, career, and leisure.

3. Ask yourself what you can leverage from your experience of making it happen. Write down all the contacts, opportunities, and experiences you gained and see how you might be able to use them for the next go around the spiral staircase.

4. Plan your confetti throwing! In your journal, write about what, where, and how you're going to fully celebrate making it happen. Make sure you light up when you write down this plan. Set a date for your celebration and put it in your calendar to make it real.

You Made It Happen!

. . . .

"Once you make a decision, the universe
conspires to make it happen."

RALPH WALDO EMERSON

M Y BIGGEST HOPE is that you benefit from reading this book and are inspired to continue on the journey of making your dreams a reality.

You could come up with a list of compelling reasons not to start something bold, brave, and daring. Likely many people around you would tell you not to start too. But when you take the steps and rise, you will be supported. People will take your hand and lift you up higher than you ever thought you could go. As you do, you'll feel light and free. You'll feel, see, and be someone new but more familiar. When you make it happen and express your true gifts, you become more of who you really are.

Making it happen is not about toiling away and working yourself into a frenzy. You have to be aware when you're forcing it to happen, and then lovingly surrender and trust. We don't know the Universe's plan for us, regardless of how much we want things to be a certain way. Making it happen is a dance between being curious, doing the work, and allowing for divinity to lift us up. We don't have to be workaholics to accomplish big things.

The Universe is constantly communicating with us in different ways—through conversations and unexpected turns of events, and by allowing us to have a vision to see things in a slightly altered way. Our job is to simply open up, listen, and receive the guidance to become our higher self. We are meant to shine brightly and this is done by letting inspiration flow through us so we can illuminate the world with our talents.

This process isn't always easy, but the best things in life never are. More than anything, the journey provides richness and texture, and yet it also feels fabulous to finally arrive at the end of a make it happen cycle. Life can flicker by so quickly if you're not conscious. You have the choice about how to spend your time.

When we allow ourselves to follow our hearts, we're never led astray. Sure, there will be many bumps and unexpected incidents that won't always seem convenient, but if you stay with your vision and trust yourself to make your dreams come true, you will have many beautiful moments of savouring the experience, knowing you made it happen.

Conclusion

. . . .

T HE FEELING OF making it happen is one of the greatest thrills you can experience in life. Whatever your big, glorious dream is, when you start to see it manifest before your eyes, a sense of wonderment, pride, and glory will fill you. Sometimes it can be overwhelming and scary, but my advice to you is to lean in to the feeling and throw your hands up in the air just like you would on a roller coaster. Life is meant to be lived to the fullest. All you can do is buckle up and enjoy the ride!

You have already learned about my experience with making it happen, so now I'd like to share advice and wisdom from the Makies themselves. I sent out an email asking: *What does it feel like when you make it happen?* The responses I received were beautiful, candid, and inspirational. Use them as rocket fuel when you get stuck along your own journey.

What Does It Feel Like
When You Make It Happen?

Making it happen is the moment when a complete rush of accomplishment floods my mind and body. Making it happen is the feeling of standing on my tiptoes, stretching my arms to the limits with all of the effort and persistence that is required to crush an almost-out-of-reach goal. Boom! Made. It. Happen.
@lacebrickdesign

When someone offers you a ride on a spaceship, don't ask what seat, just get on!
@beeswaxandcotton

What does it feel like when I make it happen? Nothing else exists. The world is my oyster and nothing can go wrong. I'm on top of the world! All the bad, all the jealousy, all the copy cats, and times I haven't been accepted are pushed aside, and I think about only my creative freedom!
@haiku.lane.handmade

Making it happen is magical. There is nothing in this world that feels so good as when you see the impact you have. I love to educate and help people. Working with Gemstones allows me to do this beautifully.
@heelerzgemstones

During the process of making it happen, it's like a steep climb and you wonder when you'll make it to the top. When it happens, you're standing on the top of the mountain and it's the most rewarding feeling in the world.
@bethandoliviahandmade

As a newbie Makie there was such a sense of excitement and apprehension. For me, Make It was a milestone moment in terms of venturing into the bigger arena of trade shows. I am far more confident now to continue in this realm.
@rchickids

Making my product allows me to be mindful and present. I find the process of stamping relaxing and I can see and feel what I have made. I just love it!!!!!
@justsimplyeclectic

Making it happen with a small business is a leap of faith. Believing in yourself, trusting your creativity and abilities feels scary at times and is all too stressful, but with that comes the excitement and the addictive thrill of someone believing in what you do. Supporting you because of what you do. That's the reward, and it's so worth it.
@villagecraftco

My life has been filled with travel photography, and now I'm overjoyed at being able to provide high-quality photographic artwork for people's spaces! I think of my art as an "affordable luxury," one my clients are inspired to look at and proud to own. I am incredibly happy that I took the leap into entrepreneurship and turned my passions into my life's work!
@lauramcglonephotography

After an unexpected breakup that left me heartbroken and financially ruined, I searched for something I was talented enough to do that might generate a little extra income. I started making caramels in my kitchen and taking them to local markets. Less than a year later, I was able to lease a commercial kitchen, hire staff, and go casual at my full-time nursing career. The empowerment and satisfaction gained going from scrounging for change to putting gas in my car to self-supporting and self-sufficiency is indescribable! I'm incredibly thankful and blessed!
@kickasscaramels

For me, creative work is fulfilling from start to finish. Even if it's something I've made before, there is still a thrill to see the finished project (and all the happy plush smiling in one big group!). Bringing an idea to life and seeing how happy it makes people just is one of the best feelings in the world. *@caseboutiquecanada*

After 10+ years of working tirelessly on my jewelry business it feels surreal to see items from my vision board become a reality. I keep a vision board of my accomplishments where I can see them because it's easy to knock something off the list, move on, and focus on what still needs to be done. I know there will always be more to do, but it feels like a dream to have been featured in major magazines, be accepted into events that took me years to break into, be profitable, and know I am growing a sustainable business. I wouldn't trade it for anything, and the journey has transformed who I am. *@andreakellydesigns*

I've been a creative "Makie" most of my life without realizing it, often experiencing bursts of intense creative energy caused by some need to resolve an issue or solve a problem. I'm often reminded that "necessity is the mother of invention," but the real gift I've realized in my life is the gift of creation by using your mind to think your way through the process, taking an idea or concept and using your own hands to make it a reality. Always keep your first prototype piece because as your following attempts continue to hit the wall just above the waste bin, you will break through to that magical "ah-ha" moment, and suddenly, there's clarity. You know what to do and voilà! you did it. There is no better sense of

accomplishment in the world. You took from your mind and created from your hands, and that's the reality that usually starts in the heart.
@insventive_sven

Before my creative partner and I started a business, we began running together. Running was a healthy activity that also allowed us time to vent and rave about being full-time caregivers. We soon discovered that both of us have a wide variety of talents beyond dealing with tantrums and meal planning, so we decided we needed to start a collaborative business. Annex Suspended Art was born and it's been a life-changing experience to help each other grow in this artistic endeavour.
@annexsuspended

Making it happen for this bird is truly feeling like a co-creator with the Universe. Inspiration flows from the Universe and we co-create. The Universe takes care of the details in providing me with the resources to manifest the idea and it feels like I am a channel and the Universe is expressing itself through me. When I'm aligned in that, it feels like the beginnings of falling in love. I eat, sleep, and breathe what I'm trying to create, and it becomes all consuming. When the creation is complete it is a pressure that has been released, a birth into the world, and finally my heartbeat can return back to normal. A sense of extreme gratitude and awe often follows as I look at the new creation, and it feels like pure magic has taken place. And then I ask for more because, damn! it feels good to make it happen!
@remindeddesigns

"Making it happen" for me means reaching those unbeliev-able dreams. Making it was getting accepted to Make It! in my first year of business. Making it is losing my primary income and knowing I could manage with the income from West Coast Leslie Designs. Making it is being able to look at all the "gold stars" I've earned that highlight what I've done with WCLD in five years. Making it will be reaching those next dreams, whatever they may be, and being prepared for the awesome adventure it will take me on.
@westcoastleslie

Even though I've been doing this for several years, I feel like I'm only still just *trying* to make it happen. Impostor syn-drome is alive and well! My customers and colleagues are so supportive though, they all make me feel like I'm on the right track towards actually making it happen.
@thedressmakerac

I've run my business for last six years and have fun with mak-ing many specialty local food products primarily made of red beets. I feel that the great satisfaction in life is: You cre-ate something unique in this world and people get attracted by it and pay for it. And that's your passion, lifestyle, and livelihood.
@drbeetrootca

There have been many times that I considered giving up or was told by others that I should, that the idea of sustaining myself through my craft was unattainable. But I refused to give up on my dreams—at every decision point along the road I chose the path that my heart wanted to follow, and

many years later it's everything I envisioned and more. I knew that if I was to have faith that the Universe would catch me, if I was going to be courageous in my approach to choosing this life, I first had to have faith in myself.
@jenimack

The life you once designed in your head slowly unfolds to be the life you actually live in!
@drizzle_honey

When I embark on a plan to make it happen I am filled with a sense of possibility and a vast feeling of the unknown . . . A creative drive to see a vision manifest to reality. . . When the vision comes together it allows me to trust that life all makes sense and I am on the right path. And I get to see beautiful things that I make shared with others!!
@shi_studio

As someone who perfected a life of procrastination, starting my own business in the busiest season of life and making it happen has changed everything. Surrounded by the beautiful chaos of family while following my dreams and letting my passion pour through is the most incredible feeling.
@naturaljacksdesign

When I opened my first storefront, it was all just so surreal. It came with an absolute flurry of excitement and new-found demands. I haven't stood still for a second since, but I absolutely love it.
@confettisweets

I'm meant to be a maker—making what I want, when I want.
No rules or boundaries. When I make it happen, I feel pure
happiness!
@simplify.ab

To make it happen is like origami, you make an investment
in nice paper and then spend time to figure out the folds—
initially there is frustration, but then something magical
happens as you watch yourself build something beautiful
and unique. You realize you have the power to create and
pass that on to other people to enjoy. What follows is almost
an addiction, because you know you can do better, and you
start to care more about what you're creating and the people
you want to share with.
@mastersoapmakers

Knowing I am keeping an ancient craft alive helps me express
my art and viewpoint and strive to be a better craftsperson.
Making a well-crafted piece of jewelry that shows my rev-
erence to the Natural World makes me feel at peace, proud,
and honoured, knowing that this is my rightful place in
this world.
@zulajewelry

You get a lot of personal satisfaction from making and selling
the product you just finished. It provides the acceptance you
need to continue doing what you love to create and make. I
also enjoy my face-to-face interactions with customers and
vendors. I love listening to their stories, challenges, and sug-
gestions to improve my product.
@lumisknittles

Through my long journey of some 27 years as a textile artist, I have learned to never give up on my dreams or doubt my decisions. Persistence and commitment are the keys to achieving your dreams. You will find success.
@mahira_murad

Before I started my own business I would have laughed at the thought of ever becoming an entrepreneur. I thought businesses were for "businesspeople" and I was the furthest thing from that! Fast forward to today and I have clients all over the world, offer wholesaling, and teach calligraphy workshops to inspire others.
@littleblacklettercompany

I really don't feel like my business has really "made it" per se by professional standards. But in this thing called life . . . it's all about experiencing "JOY" and I know my hand-lettered art brings joy into peoples' lives every day they look at it. Knowing that what I've created makes people SMILE a little brighter. By my book, that is "good enough" for me.
@secondchancescreations

As Nike keeps saying: "Just do it." You'll never know until you try. Cliché? Definitely, but so true! Don't be afraid to love other peoples' work and make connections within the maker community—you never know where you might end up. You could be sitting at your computer typing out a couple sentences for someone else's book! Ha ha!
@prairiechickprints

This year I faced my fears and stepped out into the unknown and left my job of 10 years to pursue my dream of being a jewelry designer and maker full time. Making it has fortified my belief in myself. I feel limitless in my possibilities and fearless in the face of the unknown, yet I also feel secure and content with who I am and the direction I am going in. I know that now I am the person that I've always meant to be, my soul soars with joy every time I create. What I feel most of all is happiness and for me that is what life is all about.
@the_pirate_and_the_gypsy

As an entrepreneur, when I make it happen I trust in the Universe and in the flow of life. I let go of my logistical mind and I lead with my heart. I truly believe that when we follow our bliss, everything else falls into place.
@cacao.now

Our approach has always been to make art that *we* love, art that we want in *our* home. When a product we've created brings happiness to someone, it feels like some kind of creative circle is completed: from conception of the idea, through manifestation and production, to being received into someone's home. We are always grateful for the experience, and it inspires us to do it all again!
@bigbearandthewolf

After being intimately involved in your creative process for so long—working every moment on it—for a brief moment, you may catch a reflection of your creativity in someone else's eyes or words, and you realize that you've been fully

seen. There is no greater moment than when that feeling washes over you. You are present, grounded, and whole. The feeling can be fleeting as your inner self whispers that you've barely scratched the surface and still have so much more to reveal.
@frostbitesfun

For me, making it happen = dream come true. Not only dreaming, not only talking, but taking action. It makes me feel excited, amazing, and keeps me hungry. Yup, it makes me feel more hungry for the next step in the direction of what I believe in and love.
@cyarnhut

Making it happen and deciding to follow my passion means I can make my dream a reality and enrich the lives of pets and their people! Everyone should follow their dreams and do what they love because happier people make the world a better place.
@thesharperbarker

So hard to summarize 50 years of being an entrepreneur!! My University was funded by three different business ventures, two of them involved creating art/craft items and recruiting starving students to help with production and sell them door-to-door in the well-to-do areas of Toronto. A Canadiana art store and a small furniture design/manufacturing business in Winnipeg was next, then the design and operation of an amusement park in Nanaimo. In all, 23 businesses were conceived, built, then sold over my 50-year career. I am now retired, and designing/making metal sculptures from recycled auto and motorcycle parts. Every new adventure has been a RUSH!!!

Bill Stewart doesn't have Instagram and doesn't want it! Find him at the upcoming Make It show instead ;)

Acknowledgements

. . . .

I AM DEEPLY GRATEFUL to the many people who supported me in writing this book. This journey wouldn't have been possible without all of the amazing artists and makers who I've had the privilege of getting to know through the Make It community. It's the Makies who continue to inspire my team and I to do what we do: your drive, ambition, and love for what you do has allowed the show to grow into what it is today.

A big shout out to the fierce ladies of Team Make It, especially Brigitte Stroud and Diana Luong, whose support afforded me the time, energy, and bandwidth to actually finish writing this book. As our team continues to grow, we'll always be the OG3!

I'm also thankful to everyone at Page Two who believed in my idea to write *Make It Happen*, and enthusiastically cheered me on along the way. Trena White, Gabrielle Narsted, and Kendra Ward: you've been absolute pleasures to work with.

Thank you to my dear friends who acted as sounding boards, and encouraged me to keep writing even when I wanted to stop. I appreciate everyone who took the time to read the rough manuscript and offer ideas and guidance along the way. This book is a collaborative effort of many, many, amazing conversations I've had with you all.

To Orson Stachow, who I fell in love with during the brutally agonizing editing phase: thank you for inspiring me and for being a massive cheerleader for everything I do! Your ability to make your own dream happen is one of the traits I admire in you, and I can't wait to see what we manifest together in the future.

I am grateful to my incredible parents who have been along for my crazy entrepreneurial ride since the very beginning: even though you don't always understand my vision, you have continued to support me and love me throughout it all. I appreciate all the sacrifices you've made in order to allow me to realize my dreams. I love you both so much.

Lastly, I'm grateful to Chandler: you were not only my business partner for most of my entrepreneurial journey, but also my best friend and biggest supporter. It's pretty damn surreal to think of all of the things we've created together. I'm so lucky to have been born into the same family as you because I know we challenge each other to be and do better in life. The stories in this book just wouldn't have been possible if it wasn't for you.

Sparkly love to you all!
Jenna

About the Author

. . . .

*J*ENNA HERBUT IS the creator of Booty Beltz, and her fabric sash belts have been sold by 120 boutiques all over Canada, the United States, and Japan. Booty Beltz have been featured in *Flare*, ELLE *Canada*, *LouLou*, and on *CityLine*, CTV, and Global News. After touring as a vendor in craft shows and festivals across the country, in 2008 Herbut founded and promoted her own fair, Make It, which quickly expanded to a bi-annual event in Vancouver, Edmonton, and Calgary. Make It has evolved into a well-known community for both new and established makers, and it boasts 100,000+ shoppers yearly. Since the inception of the Make It show, Herbut has expanded her business to include Conscious Lab, a community space for creative entrepreneurs located in Vancouver, Canada.

jennaherbut.com
makeitshow.ca